2/17/1

To Ms.

I so la- meeting you may rui chances of meeting you, I realize, but I had to try.

DON'T CRY FOR ME, ARDENT READER

More People, Places and Thingies from the Sacramento Business Journal

With the promise of friendship and the certainty of respect,

By Ed Goldman

BOOKS

Don't Cry For Me, Ardent Reader
People, Places and Thingies from the Sacramento Business Journal

And Now With Further Ado
*More Gravitas-Defying Profiles and Punditry
from the Sacramento Business Journal*

But I Digress
Daily Profiles and Punditry from the Sacramento Business Journal

On Goldman Pond*

How to incorporate Your Dog (and Other Solid Business Tips)*

PLAYS

Part Four of a Trilogy

Jews Don't Kayak

Friday@5
A musical, with book, music and lyrics by the author

ONLINE ONLY

Fear of Frying**
Understandable Recipes for the Cookbook-Challenged

* Published by Central Valley Press
** Published by Sacramento Magazine

DON'T CRY FOR ME, ARDENT READER

More People, Places and Thingies from the Sacramento Business Journal

Ed Goldman

Sacramento Business Journal
Sacramento, California

Published by the
Sacramento Business Journal
555 Capitol Mall #200
Sacramento, CA 95814

ISBN-13: 978-1729554869
ISBN-10: 1729554865

Printed in the United States of America
First printing — November 2018

Editors: Adam Steinhauer, Beth Davis
Cover Art by Marcy Friedman
Layout and Design by Chris Almaguer

To order copies of this book, contact the
Sacramento Business Journal at (916) 447-7661

Contents

A CAPITAL LIFE

YOUR GOVERNMENT INACTION

HOME AND HARSH

LOCAL FOCALS

PASSING THOUGHTS

A Word from the Author
(Actually, 531 Words)

Welcome, welcome, welcome, as John Oliver says on HBO's "Last Week Tonight." This is my sixth published book, and the third collection of my daily columns for the Sacramento Business Journal.

Actually, my third book, Fear of Frying, was published only online (by Sacramento Magazine). The original publisher went out of business when the book was in its final stage of proofreading. But before that happened, I did get the immense satisfaction of being paged by a desk clerk at a luxury hotel in Newport Beach, where my late wife Jane and I were attending a convention. "Mr. Ed Goldman, please see the concierge. Your publisher has sent you the proof of your new book," the clerk broadcasted. I did my best to simultaneously look mildly annoyed but nonetheless convey to onlookers in the hotel lobby that the name being paged was, indeed, mine. I couldn't see Jane's reaction since I ostentatiously bolted from her side in response to the page (which further clarified for witnesses that the page was meant for me), but I'm sure she was swelling with pride — even though it probably appeared to others that she was rolling her eyes. It's just difficult to read some people, isn't it?

This wasn't the first time one of my book deals fell through.

On assignment for Random House, I wrote a combo biography/how-to book about J. Paul Getty some years later. It, too, was in its final stage of proofing when the publisher canceled a few dozen about-to-be-published books, laid off a number of editors (including mine) and pretty much shut down its Northern California book-publishing offices. I'm surprised they didn't also tell me I could keep my wristwatch but never set it to the correct time.

This is one of the occasional comes-with-the-territory consequences of the freelance writer, for whom no one but another freelance writer has much empathy. To the outside world, it may seem that we have it made: no onerous work schedule, no holiday rumballs by Midge from Accounting to pretend to enjoy, no boss looking over our shoulder, no co-worker who thinks that saying "I'm okay — for a Thursday" is witty.

On the other hand, most of us are self-insured (if insured at all), don't have retirement plans (because that would mean we've made enough money to stop working someday) and have no idea where our next check is coming from (or if it'll arrive at all, should the publisher go belly-up).

But don't cry for me, Ardent Reader.

Writing my column for the Sacramento Business Journal since August 2011 has been the most enjoyable time I've had in my entire professional life. It sometimes surprises people to learn that I write my column under contract, as a freelance writer — but I do, and gratefully. I'm given enormous leeway in the column as long as I don't write anything hugely inappropriate and that I promise to never come into the office unannounced. Or even announced. It's an arrangement that seems to suit all of us, especially Midge from Accounting, whom I've never been able to fool about my hating her goddamn rumballs.

Ed Goldman
October 2018

Acknowledgments

I'd like to thank the following people for helping bring this book to market:

David Lichtman, publisher, and Adam Steinhauer, editor, of the Sacramento Business Journal, for allowing me to make noise five days a week online, one day a week in print and every few years between book covers. Special thanks to the SBJ's audience development director, Delania Lustig, who I'm convinced could organize Armageddon on a moment's notice and still ensure that everyone gets along.

Joe Chiodo, publisher of Sacramento Magazine, and Krista Minard, editor, for allowing us to reprint my story, "Selling Stately Goldmanor" — as well as for running my monthly column, Sacramentions, for 10 years and continuing to list (and even better, hire) me as a contributing editor.

Marcy Friedman, artist, philanthropist and regional treasure, for not only painting (and in the process, greatly improving) me — but also for allowing us to use her work here. People who've seen this painting find it hard to believe I went to Annapolis. Well, I did. And it was a wonderful weekend.

The people who read my work and those who also comment on it. I consider it a tremendous privilege that you invite me into your lives as often as you do — and, to the best of my knowledge, don't double-check the silver drawer thereafter.

My friends and family, who continue to make a very needy writer feel like a very wealthy man.

E.G.

For Kim Elizabeth

DON'T CRY FOR ME, ARDENT READER

GRAVEL AND LEISURE

Oct. 3, 2016

Driverless trucks: Coming soon to a freeway near you

Now that driverless cars are a reality — be afraid; be very afraid — the tech industry is turning its attention to driverless trucks.

The vehicles, which I've always called "trains," currently are being tested on the road. In my view, this is an excellent place to test them since ski slopes, coffee shops and saunas simply don't offer the same scientific dynamic.

So far, things are going very smoothly, according to experts and liars.

The fact that on a number of test drives, an in-transit human was urgently summoned to take the wheel moments before the truck would, say, have plunged into a mountain lake, is nothing to worry about, we've been assured. And because the driverless truck had someone inside — called, I believe, a "truck driver" — things ended well.

To be fair, some people, at least in the driverless truck industry, are touting the safety, economic and health benefits of these innovative multiton, metallic machines of death and destruction (imagine if I weren't being fair). Most of the benefits are thinly veiled critiques of truck drivers, though.

Safety? Well, a truck driver, especially if he or she is tired, can make a fatal mistake — whereas, a perfectly programmed machine won't. Tell this to my computer when it's just replicated and sent one of my emails 143 times. This was never a problem when I used a nonprogrammable typewriter or equally low-tech pen and paper.

Economic and health benefits? A tech- but not truck-industry spokesman said the other day that truck drivers will

1

be able to earn much more money because they'll be able to pick up and deliver their cargo without having to stop every nine hours to catch some winks. They'll still sleep, of course, but while the truck continues to carry the loads and them to their destinations. No more Benzedrine!

But I'm guessing there won't be too many truck drivers who'll sleep soundly as their vehicles hurtle through mountain passes and down s-curved roads. I suspect that those of us who find it difficult to sleep on planes, knowing someone up front is piloting the craft, may find it difficult to cede complete control of our survival to empty cabs.

Well, actually, Uber and Lyft already are experimenting with those. Be very afraid; be very afraid.

Airline 'free' meals may be ending

If one of your bucket-list wishes for 2017 has had you smacking your lips in anticipation of a fine-dining experience on an upcoming international flight, you may be in for some unfriendly skies.

The Wall Street Journal reports that even airlines offering luxury experiences to their business and first-class passengers, such as Air France, are looking at ways to either charge for meals (online and in advance) or eliminate them entirely.

They're doing this, they say, to compete with a bunch of economy startup airlines — one of which is owned by Air France itself. The airline is said to be watching how its Mini-Me does with pared-down amenities — and, if successful, adapt some of its strategies for the mother ships.

I'm wondering if it also plans to cut back on the extra room you receive by buying more expensive seats, thereby introducing a new amenity: Premium Leg Cramps.

I've been fortunate to fly in Air France's business class a few times — and while I loved the food, wine and Barcalounger-in-the-clouds comfort, I never kidded myself into believing that anything was being presented gratis: the cost was an unseen-by-me line item included in the sky-high ticket price.

So for the airlines to say they're contemplating charging for their currently "free" eats and beverages is a bit disingenuous — or as we also say, a complete crock, and we don't mean one filled with a savory cassoulet.

The newspaper article pointed out that some frequent flyers have been under the impression that if an international flight is of a certain duration (seven-plus hours), there's some sort of galactic law stating that the airlines must feed us. In a word, nope. If they're not overly obligated to depart and arrive on time, you can bet your escargot they don't have to provide nutrition.

I first flew across the United States when I was just shy of my fifth birthday. A flight from New York to Los Angeles in those days took about 13 hours (plus a stopover in Chicago). It was noisy, bumpy and, for many passengers, a truly nauseating experience. I'm sure they served us a meal or two but I'm not sure how many of us looked forward to it once we were airborne.

Flying today is much smoother — despite the inconvenience of TSA frisking, extra-bag fees and the off-putting development that allows the people who get on the plane in front of you to prevent you from getting to a seat as they struggle to lift and load their steamer trunks into overhead bins that have the capacity of ferret condominiums.

Even so, when most of us book flights, I'm not sure we ask what the chef's special will be that day. Our goals are more along the lines of, will we make our connecting flight, what kind of weather is expected and will the airline have someone on board to treat Premium Leg Cramps.

So, listen airlines: Stop the food service, work on the schedules and expand our legroom. The money you save on not having to wine and dine us should offset the expense you'll incur by removing some seats.

Jan. 4, 2017

Driving concerns about our car culture's slow fade

I'm a fair-weather motorhead — or at least, a situational one. I usually get excited about cars only when I need to buy one.

A few years ago, I attended the huge Barrett-Jackson auto auction in Scottsdale, Arizona, and marveled, along with my host, at how much money people were willing to spend for lovingly restored cars that had been worthless junk even when new. I'm talking about Ford Pintos, Chevy Impalas and Rambler Americans.

My dad bought a used one of the latter in the 1960s. Its radiator overheated every few miles — but since it also had reclining front seats, I liked borrowing it to ferry dates to drive-in theaters when I was in high school. This may sound like excessive sharing but in reality, the mechanism for raising and lowering the seats often jammed, resulting in either my date being driven home looking like she was in a dentist's chair or my trying to drive the car from what was, for all practical purposes, the back seat.

What's prompting this little jaunt down Nostalgia Boulevard is a recent piece in The New York Times' "Wheels" column about our culture of cars facing an uncertain future.

Many people, especially the young, no longer think of buying a car as a goal, a status symbol or even a need, according to the story. They think of it as an expense they can do without — and not just those who live in metropolitan areas, where trains, buses, traditional cabs, Uber, Lyft and bicycle lanes offer alternatives to getting to and from work and play.

Therein lies an irony. For while it's easy to tout the ecological advantage of getting cars off the road, the fact is that unless an area is urbanized enough to accommodate nondriving commuters, people still need to pilot and park their cars in order to access public transportation. One of the examples cited in the story is the Southern California city of Azusa, which "is building an old-style, car-centric solution: a 500-space parking garage" at a train stop. Yeah, that ought to clear the air.

Manufacturers are trying to address the challenge of cars no longer being gotta-haves by developing self-driving ones and even motorized suitcases, which purr along with you, R2-D2-like, if you have to walk from one mode of public transportation to another. I wouldn't like having my suitcase talk to me while I was running to catch a bus. Backseat drivers are bad enough — even if that's what you have to be when the mechanism jams in your Rambler American.

The Jetsons fly their car to Dubai

W e begin with a revised TV theme song:
"Meet Mattar Jetson!
His wife Abal!
Their son Amid!
Daughter Farhah!"

I'm having some good, clean fun with the opening of the ancient "futuristic" animated cartoon show, "The Jetsons," because the little flying car the family used to zip around in is now a reality. In Dubai.

Yes, Dubai, the little emirate that could, is introducing any minute now, and not as an experiment, single-driver flying cars. (We pause for a philosophical question: If a flying car crashes in the middle of the desert and receives no American media coverage, does it make a sound?)

OK, we're back.

Despite its eye-popping/jaw-dropping/heart-stopping wealth, I find it surprising that Dubai has beat Detroit to the airborne-auto punch.

Granted, an emirate probably has very little red tape to snip when it comes to R&D. And I imagine that obtaining a patent, copyright or approval for a new drug is less cumbersome there than here.

The emirs apparently like certain aspects of American culture. About 20 years ago, Trader Vic's (of Mai Tai fame) was one of my public relations clients. The company, which had its signature Polynesian-style restaurants in a number of major U.S. cities, suddenly found itself in a tug-of-war between two competing emirates, each of which was eager to be the first to open a Trader Vic's in its principality. It ended in more or less a tie, with Trader Vic's restaurants opening in both Abu Dhabi and Dubai in 1994.

I'm glad the sheiks focused on "The Jetsons" rather than "The Flintstones," which both came out of the Hanna-Barbera studio of hasty animation (during chase sequences, you may recall that Fred either had the world's longest house or the animators just kept repeating the background drawings to save time and money). If they had chosen the latter, Dubai's newest innovation in cars might have been one without a floorboard that you propelled with your feet, the whole while shouting "Abba Dabba Do!"

Wait. Isn't that the name of another emirate?

Welcome to the Hotel Mall-o-rama

The following may be sung to the tune of "Heartbreak Hotel," for which I apologize to the original song's writers — Tommy Durden, Mae Boren Axton and Elvis Presley.

"Well, since our business left us.
Our revenue stream's been hell.
And that is why we're opening
The Mall Hotel."
Yes, the solution to retail gloom may be retail rooms.

A number of shopping malls, stung by the fact that customers think brick and mortar stores are so last century, are trying to find ways to entice them out of cyberspace orbit and back to terra firma. They're doing it by opening boutique motels where once stood food courts, LensCrafters, video rental stores and of course jewelry, wristwatch and cellphone kiosks.

"As online channels steal business from retailers, hotels provide a retailer with a unique, direct and immediate environment to interest consumers," Henry Harteveldt of Atmosphere Travel Group told the New York Times.

This was all well and good until I read the next sentence in the story: "According to the U.S. Travel Association, a trade group in Washington, D.C., shopping was the second-most popular activity among leisure travelers, after visiting relatives."

I think the placement of the comma after "travelers" is essential in that sentence — otherwise the meaning would be that after visiting relatives, travelers like to go shopping. Whereas in my experience, after visiting relatives, most travelers like to get drunk.

If, on the other hand, it means that shopping is the second-favorite thing to do when traveling, and visiting relatives is the most favorite, then I think what we have here is something the White House's Kellyanne Conway might call an alternate fact.

Maybe it's just me, but when I travel, the second least-favorite thing I want to do is visit relatives. Oh, I love my cousins, who are the only relatives I have left besides my brother (who lives in the Monterey Bay area) and daughter. Traveling to see her now takes me about five minutes except during rush hour, when it can take as long as seven minutes. I just don't think of it as "traveling" when I visit relatives, even though a few live in Southern California and others in Vancouver, Washington. I think of it as going to see my relatives. There's no other point to the endeavor.

"Traveling," at least to me, involves sightseeing, culture observing and no one I know or will likely ever see again.

Unless I run into them at the mall.

Sacramento-to-Long Beach flight is most welcome

I was pleased to read, right here in the Business Journal, that not only is Southwest Airlines going to start offering direct flights to Long Beach (in August) but that the addition is just in time for the annual reunion of my high school drama department buddies (in September).

Over the past few years, I became increasingly annoyed that I couldn't get there from here, at least on Southwest. Apparently there was some circuitous multistop route I could take — like, from Sacramento to Phoenix to Las Vegas to Long Beach — which meant I'd be flying most of the day to get to a destination an hour away, as the (very fast) crow flies.

Some friends of mine enjoy doing this repetitive taking off and landing because it allows them to chalk up frequent-flyer miles. But for me, the only thing I'm trying to obtain when I fly is to land safely at my destination as soon as possible.

Besides, I just don't have the head for frequent-flyer math — and, in a larger sense, I realize that if I think I'll be putting one over on the airlines by devising a convoluted itinerary to save a few dollars, I have another think coming.

To me, that's akin to buying a new car and thinking the rebate offered by the manufacturer is a terrific deal ("Can you believe it? They're giving me money to buy this car!"). Or betting against the house in the aforementioned Las Vegas and thinking you'll come out ahead ("Can you believe it? They give me all the free drinks I ask for, and all I have to do is gamble away my Roth IRAs!").

Anyway, I'm looking forward to my next flight to Long Beach. In addition to the convenience, Long Beach Airport has architectural significance. If you remember the Korean War movie "M*A*S*H" — not the subsequent TV series, which ran considerably longer than the war — there's a touching moment when the character played by actor Tom Skerritt is told he's being discharged from the military. He flashes on a family reunion at an unnamed but period-appropriate airport. It's Long Beach Airport. Built in 1941, its design combines the 1930s Streamline Moderne style and what its website calls "the geometric abstraction of the post-war International Style."

I wonder if Skerritt's flight lasted more than an hour.

Aug. 13, 2018

Gift cards stolen by Sac Airport employees. Why?

A recent story in the Sacramento Bee began, "Three Sacramento-area airport workers have been indicted by a federal grand jury on charges of stealing gift cards and money from mail at Sacramento International Airport, federal officials say."

OK, stealing money I understand. Stealing bitcoin I might have. But I was shocked to learn that gift-card theft had reached such criminal proportions here as to attract the attention of the feds.

So I checked in with my "streets" adviser, an occasional inmate and somewhat clumsy pickpocket, ergo, an occasional inmate, who goes by the name Rob U. Knightley. His other aliases have included Burg L'Horizon and Ray Dior Fridge (a name he dropped after being caught in the act of stealing groceries from Airbnb kitchenettes and serving three months of a one-month sentence, an add-on due to his smarting off to the county jail's caterer).

Anyway, after I cleaned out my refrigerator as a precaution, I invited Knightley over and asked him why people would bother to steal gift cards. "You just don't understand the streets," he said, as he usually does when I ask him almost anything, even "What time are you coming by tomorrow?"

"I realize that, which is why I called you to —"

"Are you aware how many people are out there who need to drink, like, 40 lattes a day just to maintain their high?"

I confessed my ignorance — which I've become

surprisingly adept at doing after years of practice.

He went on. "Then there're the pastries, never prepared onsite yet surprisingly popular. With the right collection of gift cards, a guy could save a lot on meals. The sugar highs would be a little frightening but when you're a streets guy, you already live with an elevated pulse rate. A few maple bars or croissants ain't gonna have much impact."

I asked Knightley about other gift cards that might have lured the thieves. "Well, sure, if you like to collect desk supplies, there's the Office Depot card. There's also one you can use to load up your phone with a bunch of apps you'll probably never use, but they might provide bragging rights at a thieves convention."

After Knightley left and I restocked the refrigerator, I got to thinking that this whole enterprise reminded me of an old joke. Three guys raid a formal fundraiser and hold the attendees at gunpoint. A short while later, they leave with their loot: $50,000 in pledges.

FUNNY BUSINESS

50 jobs and titles I'll never have

I'm middle-aged only if you assume I'll live to 122. Regardless, middle age brings with it certain pleasures. I know, for example, that it's unlikely I'll be drafted into the U.S. Army at this point or asked to step in at the last minute for the star of "Sesame Street on Ice."

There's also some reckoning to do with middle age. So I reckon I'll list 50 jobs or titles I'll never have — and confess that I'm quite fine with it:

1. Writing the "Intelligent Investor" column for The Wall Street Journal.
2. Computer repairman.
3. National park docent (I love the great American outdoors but look awful in a Smokey the Bear hat. Of course, Smokey doesn't look great in my running shorts, either. And neither do I).
4. Personal trainer.
5. Choreographer for Cirque du Soleil.
6. United Nations Hmong interpreter.
7. Brad Pitt's body double.
8. Forensic scientist.
9. Nuclear physicist.
10. Whole-life insurance agent.
11. Master gardener.
12. Blue Man Group understudy.
13. White House spokesman.
14. U.S. Ambassador to any country with a name ending with "stan."
15. Kim Jong-un's hair stylist.
16. Federal court judge.

17. Beauty contest judge.
18. Pillsbury bake-off judge.
19. Motivational speaker.
20. Indy 500 champion.
21. Toreador.
22. Humvee mechanic.
23. Mayor of Bell, California.
24. Chiropractor.
25. Séance conductor.
26. Free-range chicken rancher.
27. Gluten removal consultant.
28. Bungee-jumping demonstrator.
29. Mayor of Galt.
30. Lifelong bachelor.
31. Rabbi (who wants to work Saturdays?).
32. Hand model.
33. Foot model.
34. Psychotherapist (unless that's separated into two words).
35. Uber dispatcher.
36. Nepalese Sherpa.
37. Nepalese.
38. Wealth planner.
39. Gigolo (though I like the hours).
40. Engineer (unless it's the kind who drives a train).
41. Jet fighter pilot.
42. Pilot light re-lighter.
43. Pilates coach.
44. Life coach.
45. Rugby referee.
46. Rugby spectator.
47. Rug merchant.
48. Rug wearer.
49. 35 years old.
50. A passenger in a driverless car.

IBM forces home workers back into the fold

The jig is up, and the gig is over.

IBM Corp. started recalling its work-at-home employees the other day. To define "recalling" in this instance:

1. It's not like when a car manufacturer issues recalls of a model because the gas pedal, GPS and rear-view video camera burst into flames at 45 mph.

2. It doesn't mean that IBM forgot its employees' names and is starting a management-wide memory course ("You're Midge from accounting, yes? You make those great rum balls every Christmas?").

3. It's not a reference to hitting redial on a cellphone.

What it does mean is that almost all of the people who've been telecommuting for years have to come back to the mother ship, double-quick. Recess is over, kids. It's cute how you set up your desk on an ironing board in the basement, but we've endured "20 consecutive quarters of falling revenue" even though we're the company that used to boast more than 40 percent of our employees "spent their workdays outside traditional company offices" (The Wall Street Journal is the source of those figures).

As someone who's worked at home fulltime since 1984, I must admit that IBM's decision, while seemingly cruel, is probably a good one. I didn't like people with major medical benefits pretending to be part of the gig economy, which thousands of much braver individuals than I — as well as I — have been for much of our professional lives. I've been working at home since January of 1984, for example. My daughter, born in 1986, grew up never seeing me leave for work nor return from work. I rarely even closed the door to my office. So don't tell me about transparency in the workplace!

I'm sure to offend people who have actual career jobs and work at home by saying this, but here goes: If you don't spend at least sometime at the business paying you your salary and benefits, how can you have a serious grasp on changes, trends or shifting alliances there? How can you know, except by tweet and hearsay, that there might be an opportunity for advancement — or, conversely, that what you do is being slowly phased out. These are things you sometimes pick up in the daily trajectory of workplace life. But if you don't have a strong sense of a company's interior life, how can you purport to truly understand its exterior one — i.e., its mission, which might have changed a bit over the years?

I don't claim to know anything about the daily work routine of my marketing clients. And they don't necessarily want me to. I'm good with that. It gives me plausible deniability if they're up to no good — but more to the point, I never have to sample Midge's rum balls.

Amazon, Whole Foods and drugs: Who could ask for anything more?

Almost lost in the announcement late last week that Amazon was buying Whole Foods was the simultaneous buzz about the cyber giant's desire to get into the prescription drug business.

And why not? As Ira Flatow remarked on Public Radio International's "Science Friday," this could be another example of Amazon.com Inc.'s "disrupting" of traditional business models — and, in practice, could drive down the price of drugs since Amazon would be able to negotiate with manufacturers and buy them in bulk. Or so the thinking goes.

My question: What does this do to the company's ubiquitous, personalized up-sells?

Examples:

1. "We see that you like taking opioids to treat lower-back pain, Doug. If so, you'll love 'The Panic in Needle Park.' This 1971 flick — available from amazon.com on Blu-ray, DVD, VHS, Betamax and as a live puppet show — features Al Pacino and Kitty Winn playing desperate heroin addicts (as opposed to nonchalant heroin addicts). Pop your pills, pop in the movie and get hooked. EMTs not included."

2. "We notice you've just renewed your prescription for blood-pressure pills, Doug. Why not find out how well they work by also ordering a CD of 'The Best of 2016's Campaign Speeches.' It's all here: Hillary Clinton's mention of Donald Trump's

'deplorables,' Marco Rubio's reference to the size of Trump's hands, Jeb Bush joining his audience in falling asleep during one of his speeches and Carly Fiorina explaining how she saved Hewlett-Packard by courageously leaving the company (when forced to). But wait, there's more. The big guy doesn't get off that easily. Here — on one sturdy disc that you'll want to burn copies of for your car, office computer, laptop and tablet — are more than 150 of The Donald's racist, sexist, ageist, homophobic, paranoiac slurs. (Yes, that was a busy Tuesday!) Not advised for listeners under the age of 68, over the age of 2 or those with taste or a sense of human decency."

3. "Beta blockers are one thing, Doug. What about block busters? Along with your recent subscription, why not purchase five of 2016's, loudest, most incomprehensible, box-office-loser movies. We're talking 'Deepwater Horizon,' 'The BFG,' 'Alice Through the Looking Glass' and 'Ben-Hur.' But wait! As part of your amazon.com rewards, we'll toss in Tom Cruise's 2017 cash-hemorrhaging remake of 'The Mummy.' Remember, these pairings aren't for everyone. Ask your health care specialist if beta blockers and financial disasters are for you. Stop watching the movies if they last four hours or more. And by all means, tell your doctor if you think you're dead."

Email signoffs: Are they necessary anymore?

Take care. Take very good care. As ever. Peace. Resist. Namaste.

The preceding isn't a typing exercise. It's a very brief collection of some of the email signoffs I receive from friends, relatives and business colleagues in the course of a day.

I also receive some of the following each week from readers: Keep up the good work. Thanks for writing about this. Yours in Christ. You disgust me. Hoping you go to hell shortly.

Sometimes, truth be told, both sets of signoffs mingle (as in, "Take very good care; you disgust me") but who doesn't like to mix and match?

I promise you these are genuine signoffs I've received, though I have to confess that "Hoping you go to hell shortly" was meant as a joke (I think). "You disgust me" was not (I'm certain).

I'm not sure why, in this era of casual communiqués, it's necessary to have signoffs at all. We already fumble over our salutations, with "Hi, So-and-So" or "Hey, So-and-So" seeming to be the most popular. I often start emails with "Dear So-and-So," just to be retro. I especially enjoy doing this when I respond to someone who just signed off an email to me with "You disgust me." I mean the "Dear" sincerely — in the same way that opposing lawyers in another era might have sincerely called each other "My esteemed colleague" and "My learned friend" before figuratively vivisecting them in the courtroom.

My favorite signoffs are non sequiturs, intended or not. "Yours in Christ" qualifies as one if the preceding message has been about an entirely worldly issue, for example. To me, there's no need to invoke the Prince of Peace's name (or hoped-for mutual embrace) if the matter discussed — like a request to extend a rental contract at a storage facility — had nothing to do with spirituality. The exception, I suppose, would be if someone were storing bibles or religious icons therein.

Others that used to be used in letters more frequently but never quite made the leap to emails, include: "Don't let the bastards getcha," "Floss nightly" and "Your friend, always." That last one always sounded to me like it omitted the words "Despite what we both know." But that's just my natural paranoia speaking. (I know nothing. I was out of town at the time and have receipts that prove it. So quit harassing me.)

Anyway, thanks for joining me today. Take very good care.

ARTS AND SOULS

A glance at next summer's superheroes

As summer draws to a close, we bid farewell to not only the hottest summer in the history of summers but also to the seasonal onslaught of cinema superheroes. Every other movie that opened this summer seemed to feature capes, tights, explosions and confusing "origin" stories. Many of the films lost super-buckets of money. So even though next summer's docket already is brimming with masked saviors, a cursory look at the list seems to suggest that Hollywood's running out of cash and enthusiasm.

- **X-Plainmen**: A panel of professors, wearing leotards and cunning boots under their robes and mortarboards, will attempt to unravel the bewildering back stories and crossover stories of characters in the DC Comics universe (Batman, Superman, Aquaman, the Flash, Wonder Woman) and the Marvel group of mensches (Iron Man, Spider-Man, Ant-Man, X-Men, Hugh Jack-Man). Each will tell an origin story that we'll see reenacted, for budgetary reasons, by costumed puffins. At the climax, the panel will take a vote to decide which superhero is the most super of them all. Spoiler alert: It will be Superman. That's why he's called that, for heaven's sake. He's not PrettyGoodman, is he?

- **Yonder Woman**: When is it correct to use the word "she" and when should you use the word "her" to describe a female off in the distance? Yonder Woman has the answer as she flies from city to city (in coach and when possible, on standby), descending on establishments where well-educated millennials hang out but still say things like, "Her and me get along really good." Or course they do. As I've mentioned here, functional illiteracy can be a bond.

- **Aunt-Man**: Perhaps the world's first transgender superhero, Aunt-Man shows up at public restrooms throughout the United States and just stands around making wishy-washy politicians feel edgy wondering which door he/she will enter and how they'll respond to it in the media. If this picture's a hit, a spinoff character, Uncle-Gal, may get his/her own movie and confusing origin story.

- **Stan-Man**: Stan Lee, creator of most of the Marvel characters and probably the wealthiest man to ever wear an obvious toupee, finally gets his own movie. But it doesn't turn out so well for him as all of the characters he dreamed up get together, kidnap him and demand he explain all of their origin stories, including why even the most macho of them dress like Las Vegas showgirls. At the end, Lee is rescued by Donald Trump and a new set of superheroes, The Dubious Hair Brigade. "Those of us whose daily cosmetics include Super Glue have got to stick together," Trump whispers to Lee — needlessly adding, "Pun intended. I can be a very funny guy. Probably one of the funniest you'll ever meet. Listen to me. ..."

Sept. 30, 2016

'Ask Joey' Garcia has been answering for 20 years

Joey Garcia, whose impressive height, stature and runway-model posture have been turning heads all of her adult life, says, "I finally stopped growing at the age of 20."

I beg to differ — and so, I imagine, would the many thousands of readers who've been religiously reading her "Ask Joey" advice column in the Sacramento News & Review for the past 20 years. I'm one of them. And if you follow her work or chat with her for a couple of hours, you discover a seeker who doesn't intend to stop growing.

"I think people like what I have to say because I'm not someone who thinks there's only one way to live your life," she says over a recent lunch. "Having children's one way to live; not having children's another way. Same with being married or not being married. Reality is much more free than that. There are so many ways to live and do well."

Garcia, who'll turn 56 early in November, doesn't look or act appreciably older than her most persistent demographic — the millennial, X and Y generations to whom SN&R's irreverent but politically tuned vibe is pitched. On the other hand, "I get letters from some very senior citizens," she says. "Even if they're in nursing homes, they're still trying to deal with relationships."

Her book, a compilation of her columns, is titled "When Your Heart Breaks, It's Opening to Love." The clarifying cover descriptor is "Healing and finding love after an affair, heartbreak or divorce." Know anyone who could possibly relate to any of that?

29

Garcia's not a licensed therapist, psychologist or counselor. She majored in political science and journalism, a joint major, at California State University Sacramento. She nabbed a big private-sector job while still in her 20s — she was general manager of the public relations department at Ogden Martin Systems, a multinational energy corporation — but says, "My heart was in other things." She taught school, worked as a journalist in print, radio and television in the Bay Area and taught educational programs on relationships at private and public workshops.

All of which begs the question: Why's she so good at giving advice?

"Life experience," she says, smiling. "If you have relationships and pay attention, you don't have to fall apart if they don't work out. You have to figure out what you learned, trust in God and move on."

Born in Belize and raised in Hayward, California, Garcia occasionally encounters readers who assume "Joey" is a guy, even though the photo that runs with her column clearly indicates otherwise. One reader in particular thought Joey Garcia was a very sensitive Latino and was a tad unclear who the woman in the photo was. (My suspicion is that this reader was a tad unclear about other things as well.)

Garcia's book is a refreshing and fast-paced read. I enjoyed its upbeat message and occasional sass ("Shrink your dating pool," she advises someone who takes a flyer on a long-distance romance and discovers that, as a couple, the two have zero in common).

This exchange is my favorite: "Dear Joey, I cannot stop thinking about my ex-boyfriend who recently married. Can you help me forget and be happy for him?"

Garcia replies: "Yes! He is not the man for you! How do I know? Because he married someone else!"

If that sort of straight-from-the-shoulder suggestion is

what you need, Garcia will conduct a workshop on Thursday, Oct. 13 called "Love Like a Boss!" I plan to attend. I see it as an opportunity to grow with the help of someone who has no intention of stopping.

Paul McCartney speaks

Tomorrow evening, I and 17,000 of my closest friends are scheduled to see Paul McCartney make his Golden 1 Center debut in the first of two concerts. What you may not be aware of is that I was able to score a backstage interview with McCartney prior to the first concert, but it came with conditions:

1. I would be "backstage" in the sense that I'd be a few blocks behind the building.
2. We'd conduct the interview by text, and he'd never have to look at me.
3. He would answer my questions only by using the titles of songs he'd written or co-written.

I readily agreed to the terms.
Excerpts of our faceless chat follow:

ME: Hi, Paul!

PAUL: Hello, Hello!

ME: Since I can't see you, what are you doing right this moment?

PAUL: Fixing a Hole.

ME: In the roof of the new arena? When did that happen?

PAUL: Yesterday.

ME: What are you using?

ARTS AND SOULS

PAUL: Maxwell's Silver Hammer.

ME: I see. Well, as you know, I'm a —

PAUL: Paperback Writer.

ME: Well, yes, the Business Journal's published a couple of collections of my —

PAUL: Say, Say, Say.

ME: You're right. This is about you, not me. You know what I'm here for?

PAUL: Drive My Car?

ME: I wish. How cool would that be? No, as you mentioned, I'm a writer and my column appears —

PAUL: Eight Days a Week.

ME: Feels like it sometimes. Actually, I just write six —

PAUL: Let It Be.

ME: Good point. Sorry. I'm just so excited to chat. Are you glad you're doing this interview?

PAUL: I Should've Known Better.

ME: What would have made this worse?

PAUL: If I Fell.

ME: Oh, you mean when you were fixing that hole?

PAUL: Help!

Cinemark theaters are like airports

I was only partly kidding as I asked a cashier at the spectacular new Cinemark movie complex on Ethan Way what time my flight leaves.

The once-familiar centipede-like gaggle of theaters now feels like a modern airport, complete with ticket scanning.

I went there two nights in a row — the first time to see "LaLa Land," which I loved, the second to see "Rogue One," which kind of exhausted me. My inner little boy still loves shoot-'em-up westerns, with the profound exception of "The Hateful Eight," perhaps the worst written of Quentin Tarantino's adolescent compost heaps. ("Look, I can have everyone say the N-word over and over and pass it off as authentic to the time period. May I have some more soda? Soda! Now!") But two hours of watching stuff get blown up is a bit enervating. There is, however, a final shot in "Rogue One" that's heartbreaking in light of recent celebrity news but I don't want to spoil its impact for you.

I also was amazed at how the film brought back the late actor Peter Cushing, who was in the original 1977 "Star Wars," via some very clever, undetectable computer wizardry. It's not as though Cushing died on the set while making this film, and they just had to do some fill-in work; he died 23 years ago. (If you're into ruining the magic for yourself, check out The New York Times story about how they did it.)

But let's get back to the new Cinemark cinema complex and its airport-like features.

The cinema's seats were another air-travel touchstone for me. They are like the recliners you melt into if you fly business- or first-class on Air France — La-Z-Boys in the sky. The seats have cup holders and can be adjusted to what seems like a few ergonomic positions. This can be problematic. If you feel so much like you're in your own den, you can easily nod off — especially if you're just not into watching stuff get blown up.

There's also a makeshift cafe in the lobby, in case you're smart enough to realize the advertised 6:30 p.m. show time is an utter fabrication. Grab your seat at 6:30, and you'll be in for about 30 minutes of trailers, TV commercials, reminders about not using your cellphone and an ad that reminds you just how lucky you are to be in a Cinemark theater. It reminded me of David Letterman's saying that a movie a guest on his show was there to plug would be opening "in select cities" that weekend. "I can only pray to God your city will be selected," he told the audience, or words to that effect.

Torpidity seems to be the main objective at the new complex. The lobby food is heavier than it used to be (warm pretzels with nacho dipping sauce, anyone?), and the only physical activity you get is walking to your particular screening room.

I'm sure it won't be long before Cinemark or another luxury theater chain fixes that by adding people movers.

Well, gotta run. They just called my flight.

Quinn Hedges: State worker by day, singer-songwriter by night

I need to apologize in advance for announcing the world premiere of a movie Thursday evening that's already sold out — at the Blue Oaks Century Theater in Rocklin, the entertainment capital of Placer County (unless you factor in Auburn, Roseville and Loomis).

The good news is that singer-songwriter Quinn Hedges says the film — which he's yet to see in its completed form, even though it's a compilation of music videos for his new album — will probably migrate to YouTube pretty quickly thereafter.

Hedges, 37, spent three years producing the album. He performs about 100 times a year in area "nightclubs, restaurants, wine bars and at weddings," he said last week over a late-afternoon coffee in a North Natomas Starbucks, a few yards from his day job. For nine years, he's been a licensing analyst for the California Gambling Control Commission. For three years before that, he worked as a claims adjuster for the Division of Workers' Compensation, which is part of the state's Department of Industrial Relations.

If these don't exactly sound like the kind of positions that spawn rock poets, you should check out Hedges' work at quinnhedges.com. His songs are lyrical, mostly upbeat and eminently danceable. (My fave on the album is, "You Don't Even Know," but there are plenty of catchy tunes to choose from.)

The CD, entitled, "Slightly South of Stormy Clouds," is a family affair. His dad, Bernie Hedges, a guitarist who did a lot of "gigging" in his earlier years, can be heard playing. He's also Quinn's go-to guy for any tech problems with amps and guitars. His mom, June, a longtime singer, does vocal backgrounds. "I always try to sneak my family into my work," Hedges says with a grin. In addition, his cousin, John B. Hedges, did the music arrangements and coproduced the album with Quinn.

Hedges says he started writing songs when he was 18, after "a breakup. I was feeling really down so I just started writing about it. It helped heal me. It provided closure, and I never looked back."

Despite being armed with a bachelor's degree in jazz studies from Sonoma State University, Hedges says his early jobs, bartending and giving tennis lessons, just weren't paying enough and took too much time to allow him to play his music. A friend told him about job openings at the state. "He said, 'You've got a degree. They'll hire you.' I said, 'It isn't exactly in a field they're looking for,' and he said, 'A degree is a degree.' So that's how I got in, and I've been very grateful for it."

Hedges and his wife, Davita, an emergency room nurse, have been together "five-plus years," he says. The couple welcomed their first child, Liam James Hedges, into the family band almost eight months ago. I ask Hedges if Liam has exhibited any tendency toward music. He laughs. "No, not yet," he says, "but I'm trying a psychological experiment on him. Whenever I change his diaper, and afterward he's all clean and happy, I play and sing to him. If I'm right, it'll make him associate music with feeling good."

Meet Liz Bagatelos,
master makeup artist

"I'm completely Italian," Liz Bagatelos says as she joins me for lunch at Fins Market & Grill the other day. Getting here was a short commute for her: Calkin/Boudreaux Dermatology Associates, the dermatology clinic where she works as an esthetician (and also sees her own makeup clients), is just across the street on Fair Oaks Boulevard. "I jaywalked!" she announces as though confessing to a major felony.

Bagatelos is spirited and funny. Her parents and grandparents were Italian (which explains her opening remark). She readily volunteers her age, 49, saying in a mock brag, "Why not? I'm a good ad for taking care of your skin!" That she is: Dark eyed and olive complected, she looks at least 15 years younger. You'd certainly trust her to advise you on your own blemishes.

Her expertise extends well beyond that, though. Bagatelos was a longtime member of the highly regarded Style Army created by stylist Mary Gonsalves Kinney and San Francisco photographer Laurie Levenfeld, and worked on a number of ad campaigns, principally for print. She's also done the makeup for executives and the boards of corporations and nonprofits for photo shoots — and, notably, for former Gov. Arnold Schwarzenegger, who, she says, contrary to his image, "was always a perfect gentleman to me, always businesslike." She adds that he was relatively easy to prepare for the camera: "He's taken amazingly good care of his skin and himself."

Bagatelos says her private clients, most of whom are

38

women, cover a mixed demographic. "I work with East Sac moms in their 40s and up, and brides-to-be in their 20s and 30s," she says. She generally visits clients at their homes though some come to the clinic. Among her specialties are eyebrow shaping, spray tanning ("No one should lie in the sun anymore. Period!") and, what intrigues me during our chat, "tattoo camouflaging."

"You can't get rid of a tattoo entirely except through surgery," she says, "which the clinic does. But when someone has a special event to go to, like her own wedding, they think they'll be embarrassed if they wear a dress that's at all revealing." Bagatelos says she gets out her color wheel — I think she seems too knowledgable to mean this literally — and covers up the tattoo's colors with their opposites on the spectrum. "The opposite of red is green," she explains, "so if someone has a tattoo consisting mainly of red, I'll put on green makeup." She sings the praises of Dermablend, a product that seals the makeup enough so that even if the client perspires, her secret will remain safe — at least long enough to get through the event in question.

Bagatelos and her husband, Jon, who's in commercial real estate, have been together 24 years. They have three children: Domenika ("Nika"), who's 15; Giovanni ("Gio"), who's 11; and Bianka, who's seven "and is pretty much in charge," her mom says.

Bagatelos is a bit of a night owl, something I found out when she and her husband bought my home last Thanksgiving and she began texting me late at night asking questions about the house's many and confusing electronic and design features. I had never met her during the sales process; it was afterward, when I began to receive her messages, some of which were hilarious, that I Googled her and was intrigued by her background. Ergo, this interview.

I ask her at lunch if, with her fast-talking, always-moving personality she considers herself a Type A personality. In a nanosecond, she says, "No. Type-Crazy!" And, of course, completely Italian.

Trial lawyer Joe Genshlea brings his one-man show to STC

When Joe Genshlea walks onto the Sacramento Theatre Company stage later this month, don't believe the ads that call this a "one-man" show. Oh, Genshlea will be alone up there, all right. But what you'll get for the price of admission are the humor, wisdom and insights of a celebrated trial attorney, a professional mediator, an author and a raconteur — all rolled up into a tallish, elegant man in his late 70s whose blue eyes still sparkle like those of a mischievous 14-year-old. (In fact, some of his stories place him at about that age — and younger, and older.)

"Following My Nose: A Memoir of an Undirected Life," scheduled for 8 p.m. Oct. 28 and 2 p.m. Oct. 29, is Genshlea's third show about growing up in California's capital. As he likes to point out, he still lives a few yards from his childhood home in the Land Park area near Sacramento City College.

The show, which will be on STC's main stage, is a fundraiser for the playhouse, as was his first one, "A Sense of Place," which was performed in the Wells Fargo Pavilion (the Music Circus venue that shares the block with STC). His second show, "Son of 'A Sense of Place,' " was staged at the Crest Theatre. Both were popular, and at least one is available on DVD.

I've been fortunate to play a teensy role in all three shows — though, rest assured, not on stage. I think Genshlea and I decided I'm his story consultant as well as friend, roles that have led to my listening to his quite wonderful, frequently hilarious and unexpectedly moving tales, then saying something trenchant like, "Oh, that's a good one, Joe. Oh, definitely use that one." I'm also listed as "barely" directing the show. I took the same credit for the second show, and both may be examples of overstatement.

It's worth noting that Genshlea's shows aren't nostalgia wallows. While he still looks fondly on the relative simplicity of life here in the 1940s and onward, he has very strong views about things that have changed for the better (science, medicine and gender acceptance make more than cameo appearances in the new production).

The unsung hero of these show biz forays has been Genshlea's wife of many years, Barbara Como. She's not only helped with every aspect of planning the show but has offered her court reporting skills (she owns a business that does the same) to help shore up the scripts and stories. For the first two shows, I recorded Genshlea telling me his stories; Como transcribed our sessions practically overnight. Talk about an instant script.

For anyone who grew up in Sacramento — or moved here and felt as though you'd entered a theater after the film had started — I think you'll find this new show illuminating, thought provoking and, at times, sidesplitting.

Writers event comes to River City

"We have a thriving writers community here," Nancy Teichert says during a recent lunch interview. "I'm not sure enough people know that. But it's a real plus for the region."

She should know. Involved with the Community of Writers at Squaw Valley group for years, she's excited about the nonprofit organization's co-hosting an event on Nov. 11 right here in River City. Bestselling author Janet Fitch ("White Oleander") will be chatting onstage at 7 p.m. with Capital Public Radio's host Beth Ruyak at CLARA, the school-turned-arts facility at 1425 24th St.

Teichert is a longtime friend and former neighbor (I left the nabe; she didn't). She's a Pulitzer Prize-winning journalist, in the public service category, for work she did at The Clarion Ledger in Jackson, Mississippi. She's also a former Sacramento Bee reporter, who retired in 2006 after 25 years. She spent a number of her early retirement years caring for her father-in-law, husband Fred's dad, Henry Teichert. When Henry passed away four years and four days ago at age 96, she plunged herself into working on her own writing and being part of the community of fellow practitioners she lauds.

"Everyone talks about our arts community," she says, "and I'm glad that's attracting attention. But we also have some wonderful writers in the capital region, and they need to support each other." The Squaw Valley writers collective has been around for nearly half a century. That it's holding a major event in Sacramento — in collaboration with Stories on Stage Sacramento — is, Teichert says, "indicative of how many writers and lovers of writing are here."

Author Fitch, the special guest, will be talking about her new historical novel, "The Revolution of Marina M.," whose backdrop is the period when the tsarist regime was overthrown. The book-signing event will feature "Russian sweets and vodka," Teichert says, as well as Russian and Eastern European music performed by Beaucoup Chapeaux.

As further evidence of the emergence of a true writers community in Sacramento, Teichert and I are joined at the lunch byJennifer Basye Sander, a former editor at Random House (she was mine, in fact), and the author of a number of books, most notably "The Complete Idiot's Guide to Getting Published," now revised and in its fifth edition.

Sander founded and ran Write By The Lake, a writing retreat at her Lake Tahoe vacation home, and Write at the Farm (her family's) in the Skagit Valley of Washington. The former will run until the end of 2017, she says. "I'll post new dates on my website for November but from 2018 on, I will only do it up in Washington." She says she plans to attend Teichert's Nov. 11 event at CLARA. So do I. And if you like to read or write or do both, so should you.

Oct. 20, 2017

Meet Amy Seiwert, incoming artistic director of the Sacramento Ballet

Amy Seiwert, the new artistic director of the Sacramento Ballet, says the career life of a dancer can be measured out in dog years. Meaning, one of ours equals seven of theirs. "I am therefore 102," she proudly announces with an ear-to-ear grin at lunch.

Don't bother to do the math. Seiwert is 47 and retired as a dancer — eight years of which she spent at the company she'll now run — when she was 38.

Seiwert is from a musical family, "a long line of piano teachers. I grew up playing piano and oboe and singing," she says. Her aunt, Karin Baker, was a choreographer for Broadway shows. She was working as Gower Champion's assistant choreographer on the show "42nd Street," when Champion died just 10 hours before the opening night performance. The producer, David Merrick, asked the family to keep it a secret, especially from the cast, until the final curtain, when he walked on stage and told the shocked audience and company what had happened (this is why Merrick was known as a master showman — which, you can see, is not always a compliment). Seiwert's aunt took over Champion's duties; the show ran for almost a decade. "This is in my blood," Seiwert says.

Her plan for the next season of the Sacramento Ballet will be pretty much under wraps until she officially takes over on July 1, 2018 — which, one can imagine, could be a cause for discomfort. The ballet's board of directors didn't renew the contract of husband and wife Ron Cunningham and Carinne Binda, the company's co-artistic directors for the

45

past 29 years, yet the couple is still working on the current season.

Meanwhile, Seiwert has been dropping by to meet the dancers and talk to the board's just-appointed chairman, Andrew Roth, whose day job is working as the benefits and services executive officer for the California State Teachers' Retirement System. The day we speak she's just spent a morning watching dozens of children audition for "The Nutcracker," Cunningham's signature production. In an earlier conversation, Seiwert said she thought it likely he'd be brought back as a guest choreographer to map out the show after she takes over. "I watched the little kids audition for the baby mice" roles, she says with a smile. She shakes her head a little. "It was nice to have a window into how a production of this size works. Ron certainly knows how to work with kids, and he's created a well-oiled machine."

While she needs to remain mum about it until budgets are created and reviewed, she allows that her first season as artistic director will include at least one brand-new work, "probably early in the season."

Her arrival has fueled some mild controversy, principally because the Cunninghams are a local institution and, as another board member told me, not for attribution, "Their dismissal wasn't handled as well as it might have been."

No one has faulted Seiwert, however, whose credentials are eye-popping. She danced with the Sac Ballet from 1991 to 1999 and later spent eight years as the in-house choreographer for the justly celebrated and adventurous Smuin Ballet. (This isn't hype: I've seen some of their shows over the past 10 years, including the sexiest Christmas ballet I've ever seen — though I'll concede that there aren't many sexy Christmas ballets to compare it to.)

Seiwert and her husband, Darren Johnston, a trumpet

player and composer who studied musical composition at Mills College, have been together 12 years. Since the two have been based in the Bay Area, they're still working on the logistics of where they'll make their home (or homes) once Seiwert's here full time.

But one thing that isn't up in the air is Seiwert's enthusiasm for the future. "This is my dream job," she says, "though it's not the situation I would've wanted to begin it. I think the dust will settle, and we'll do some wonderful things."

Artist Jeff Myers displays a burst of new works

J eff Myers has been a professional painter since he was 15 years old. Now 49, he's a veteran of major and minor solo and group shows, and pretty serious sales, throughout the region as well as on that little make-it/ break-it island called Manhattan (and not the one in Kansas, Dorothy).

Yet, as he approaches his first solo show here in nearly three years — "Larger Than Life," composed of 30 new works at Elliott Fouts Gallery on 19th and P streets — he's still filled with the childlike enthusiasm of a talented newcomer.

This may be what happens when you're the only child of a beloved creative couple, Sally and the late Tom Myers, who together built the most exhaustive library of brilliant and often-used stock photography in the region. They were friends of mine for many years (and Sally still is). One day, when I went to their Land Park home (which I recall as having file cabinets throughout the house), to purchase some photos of Sacramento landmarks for a marketing client, the two pulled on hand puppets of a priest and nun and had them engage in a (literal) fist-fight on my behalf — in the living room. They were in their 70s at the time. I can't begin to tell you how tickling it was to be in the orbit of septuagenarians who refused to act their ages. (Tom Myers died a few years ago at the age of 88.)

Jeff — whom I knew slightly when he was a kid, and whose parents all-but-idolized him — has maintained that spirit of adventure and whimsy. Some of the collages in his new show, as well as his self-portrait, feature photographs of models with images of aerial photos of roads, farms, railroad tracks and urban grids superimposed on their nude bodies. But this isn't post-production magic, in which a computer would have combined separate images of the bodies and photos. Instead, Myers had the models "stand very still" as he projected (with five different projectors) the aerial pictures onto them, then photographed and painted the hybrid image. The results are funny and scary at the same time — but also, to my eye, compelling and oddly beautiful.

"For the past 10 years, I've had this inspiration to combine photography with oil (painting)," Myers says over cocktails at the original 33rd Street Bistro in East Sacramento one late afternoon. "I'm kind of a Zen guy. Since you already may feel that amazing redwood tree (you're looking at) in your chest, why not show it that way?"

Myers is married to Sonja Jimenez, with whom he's lived "for at least 15 years." He laughs. "Don't get me in trouble for not knowing the exact number. All I know is that it's been amazing." Jimenez recently has created, and runs, an acupuncture program for Sutter Health.

Myers says he "grew up on dirt roads. I spent a lot of time with my dad on photo shoots, and he didn't think there was anything not worth a look. He was the most curious individual I've ever known. He used to say, 'Why read books on philosophy when you can create your own?' He meant by just looking at things, listening and living your life."

It's a wonderful legacy, artist's statement and credo — and may describe the collage that's Jeff Myers.

Retired surveyor Kevin Akin creates finely crafted violins

Kevin Akin worked for 22 years as a land surveyor for the California Department of Transportation, an exacting job that requires patience and attention to details. In retirement he's been relaxing as a violin and cello maker — an exacting job that requires patience and attention to details.

Akin, 62, is a tall man with a strong grip and easygoing demeanor. He grew up in Joseph, a small rural town in Oregon where, he says, "I lived my life outdoors, hunting and fishing." His work as a surveyor also kept him outdoors for most of his career.

These days, though, he spends a lot of time inside — either in his immaculate shop or what he calls his "incredibly messy garage" where he creates instruments made in the style of Stradivarius violins and cellos. He spent four-and-a-half years studying the craft (and history of same) at the clearly named Violin Making School of America in Salt Lake City, Utah. He holds a certificate as a luthier — an artisan who builds and services string instruments. "I do some repairs," Akin says modestly. His final exam at the school required students to make two violins from scratch in just three months.

On Monday of this week, I visit the home he shares with his wife, Beverly — an artist and retired speech and language pathologist — and three cats on a quiet street in Fair Oaks. To me, Akin's "messy garage" looks like Santa's workshop before it gets cleaned up for annual photo ops and holiday cards. Lathes, saws and a full complement of gouges, chisels and hand-planes are sitting idly during my visit but appear ready for action the moment I leave.

In the relatively short time he's been plying his trade, Akin already has sold a cello and a violin to a specialty store in San Francisco. His current inventory includes five finished violins and six others that are nearing completion. The finished ones are gorgeous, with "mostly maple sides, back and neck, a spruce top and ebony pegs," Akin says as we look through the protective case in which he stores them. The price range is $2,500 to $3,000.

He's currently working on what he calls "a quartet: two violins, a viola and a cello." While he clearly puts his own imprint on his work, he works from blueprints called posters. "I'm not going to make an exact copy of what's in the designs," he says, "but I realize I can only push these boundaries so far."

I ask him what's the biggest impediment to selling his work, and he smiles. "No one knows me or my name," he says, "and I'm still alive."

While he has yet to put up a website, you can contact this otherwise modern guy —who's also a throwback to an era of handmade, exquisitely rendered musical instruments — at kaviolins@gmail.com. No strings attached.

Franklin Kakies offers
a design for living

Franklin Kakies is a respected residential interior designer — and, as he says ruefully, "one of the region's best-kept secrets." He does very little self-promotion — and many of his clients, who range from comfortable to quite affluent (but in all cases, very private) fear if they talk him up too much, he'll no longer be available to them.

I've been to two of the homes he worked on, and I've reviewed much of his portfolio. He's a combo and a curio: a classicist in his love of design history but also ultramodern when it's called for. "I like to design and decorate so that whatever things are thrown into the mix, the finished room or home will look like it's absolutely appropriate for today as well as the period of (the) original design."

As lithe as a ballet dancer, which he once aspired to be, Kakies lives in a smallish home in South Sacramento that overflows with paintings, sculptures, tchotchkes, photos, period lamps (a particular passion of his) and stylishly timeless furniture he's upholstered and reupholstered over decades rather than sell or give away. This is where he lived with and cared for his mother, one of his most enthusiastic champions, in her later years.

The home seems an extension of Kakies' personal charm "and my wry humor" (he says wryly). On a dreary afternoon, with the clouds playing peek-a-boo with the sun, he serves us cups of hot Russian black tea in exquisite cups only a tad larger than demitasses, and madeleines, the doughy cookies that figure so prominently in Proust's "Remembrance of Things Past." I mention this because Kakies has mentioned it as he puts out the plate — and because he's one of the few designers I've met who thinks of books having a use beyond smartening up a den's décor.

Kakies was born in Denver, but moved to Sacramento when he was 4 ½ years old. His father, Hans, first worked for the Veterans Administration in Colorado, then accepted a job as a clinical psychologist with the California Youth Authority. His mother, Monica, owned Happy Corner Nursery School. "My parents were political refugees who worked for the resistance," he says.

They "both worked with a small group of Germans, in Germany, speaking out against Hitler before he came to power, trying to alert their fellow countrymen to the danger he posed," he continues. "Because of their beliefs they had to flee, literally to save their lives. Mother escaped to Paris via Vienna, and eventually, after Paris fell, they met up in the unoccupied zone of France."

His mom escaped across the Pyrenees to Lisbon where she got passage to America. "My father's case was more difficult, though," he says. "As a German national of military age, he was forced to escape through North Africa to Cuba, where he was jailed on suspicion of being a Nazi.

"Mother managed to retain a lawyer to plead his case, and they were married — in Reno of all places — the moment he officially set foot on American soil. It's quite a story." Kakies' given name is a tribute to Franklin Delano Roosevelt, whose immigration policies allowed his parents to establish themselves as American citizens. His father died when Franklin was just 7 years old.

Kakies holds a master's degree in art (painting and sculpting) from California State University Sacramento, which he earned during the school's glory days as a magnet for prominent artists/professors such as Jack Ogden, Ruth Ripon and Gerald Walburg. He shows me one of his own paintings (it's a wonderful impressionist piece, which I would buy in a heartbeat) during a brief tour of his home, and I ask why he stopped painting. "I actually don't know," he says after a pause. "Maybe I'll start again."

In the meantime, you can check out some of his interior designs at his website, franklinjohnkakies.com. He deserves to be more than "one of the region's best-kept secrets."

Remembering Russ Solomon's wink

L ike so many of you, the passing of Russ Solomon on March 4 — while hooting at someone's outfit on the telecast of the Oscars and awaiting a refill of his whiskey, according to his son, Michael — left me sad but also smiling a little.

Here was a guy who'd lived a very full and colorful life, whose booming basso profondo voice was a clarion blast of optimism and self-confidence, and whose antics — like cutting off the bottoms of their neckties when stuffy visitors dropped by during his wildly successful years — were anarchistic but relatively harmless (unless it was your necktie and you'd spent a lot of dough on it).

What may be getting downplayed in the outpouring of tributes and recollections, including a fine story in the New York Times, is that Solomon, for all his international business adventures, never stopped buying the work and boosting the careers of local artists in almost every field. The showcase home he shared with his lovely and loving wife Patti was an indoor/outdoor art gallery filled with the art of Northern California painters and sculptors.

Solomon also assisted local authors. He hosted a book signing for me at Tower Books both on Broadway and at the Country Club Plaza outlets when my first collection of columns, "How to Incorporate Your Dog, and Other Solid Business Tips," was published in 1987. I had met him only moments before the Broadway event and was probably blushing and gushing with gratitude. I grabbed his hand to shake it and was surprised at how noncompetitive his grip was — as you may know, some guys turn a simple handshake into a test of manliness — and how affably humble he was.

"Well," he said in a low murmur, "I like local authors." Then he grinned. "And, frankly, the title of your book made me laugh." To me, this was like winning the Nobel and Pulitzer prizes in one gasp since I presumed that Solomon's vast knowledge of music extended to literature. I never did find that out and really didn't care. I knew immediately he hadn't read my book, just that he thought the title was funny. And that I was a local writer. And that was good enough for him and certainly good enough for me.

In fact, Solomon had an entire section of each Sacramento store dedicated to the work of local writers, which was exciting and daunting since when I looked over some of the other books there, I realized my own work completely lacked the gravitas of those. It was like being asked to sit at the grown-ups' table for the first time.

In the succeeding years, I got to know Solomon a bit more, especially as I started collecting original art in as determined a way as my meager financial resources would allow. At his home, I was thrilled to find that he had bought the art of some people I collected, too. We talked about our favorite artists a few times, and I loved the fact that we had the same childlike enthusiasm for others' creativity.

About two years ago, when I was president of Blue Line Arts in Roseville, the gallery's curator, Tony Natsoulas, put on a show of some of Solomon's collection. My job was to interview Solomon on the opening night, and I found him to be hilarious. The more esoteric my questions, the more deadpan blunt were his replies. I thought maybe I was being pretentious (I still think maybe I was), and he must have seen the look of embarrassment in my eyes as his myth-shattering answers kept getting laughs.

Then he did something that only I could see: With his "upstage" eye, the one only I could see when he was in profile, he gave me a most reassuring wink. He was having fun. He was cutting off my necktie. In essence, he was saying that life was too serious to be so serious. And this is the darling man I'll always miss.

March 21, 2018

Stephanie Taylor celebrates 50 years of work by working some more

Stephanie Taylor tells me she's "never earned a living as an adult that wasn't in the field of art." I ask her if she ever considered teaching it. "I don't think I like people enough," she says with one of those half-crooked smiles for which someone invented the word "enigmatic."

You have to spend a little time with Taylor — whom I and many others consider to be an important California artist who's sometimes overlooked because much of her work in the past 50 years has been for industrial or commercial clients — to realize this may be more of a tossed-off remark than a serious self-assessment.

Which is not to suggest that candor doesn't play more than a supporting role in her life. But since she's been an in-demand artist for half a century, accepting commissions from around the world, you suspect they've required her to play well and get along with others. Those others are very high-powered clients that include the powers-that-be at Disney and the famous Roosevelt Hotel in Beverly Hills, for which she created many paintings before the place changed hands (more than once) and the art did a vanishing act.

Closer to home, Taylor's worked (or is working) on projects for Jackson Properties, Otto Construction, the California State Railroad Museum, the Sacramento Public Library, the Sutter Club, Beers Books, the Marketplace at Birdcage mall, the Bread Store, Lyon Village Shopping Center, Raley Field and the Sacramento Zoo, among many others.

Her "Big Fish" sculpture adorned the now-closed Scott's

Seafood in Loehmann's Plaza and now welcomes you to the restaurant's much more enticing location on the Sacramento River. She also created a giant portrait of author Jack London that adorns the east side of Beers Books on S Street.

And if you've headed east on J Street from downtown, you've no doubt seen her take on Charles Nahl's "Sunday Morning in the Mines" on the west-facing wall of the Masonic Temple at 11th Street. It's a playful spin on the classic 1872 oil, owned by the Crocker Art Museum, to which she's added some guys climbing a ladder to get into the painting (or climbing down to get out of it). This is one I always point out to visitors because it shows that one of Sacramento's most endearing traits is its relative lack of self-seriousness.

"I originally wanted to be an architect," Taylor says over a recent lunch. "I like the epic scale of it." It's not a surprising comment when you realize that she considers her large-scale projects as "art in architecture"— installations (which she often personally engineers) and murals that fit in with and frequently enhance a building's design.

Take the piece she has at 333 University Ave., "Drop By Drop," which Taylor says is "the biggest installation of my career." It's quite amazing. In an immaculate commercial building with Art Deco undertones owned by Jackson Properties, Taylor sculpted "around 5,000 elements" that look like ceramic raindrops and suspended them from a 24-foot ceiling. The result is that when you walk into the lobby, you feel as though you're doing a cameo in one of Alexander Calder's famous mobiles.

Tomorrow: A closer look at the artist and her art. Don't touch the oils!

March 22, 2018

For the first 36 years of her 50-year career, Stephanie Taylor was principally a painter and muralist. In 2004, she decided to go back to college (California State University Sacramento) to study sculpture. Fourteen years and many commissions later, she says she did it because, "It's always been really important to me to stay one step ahead of the curve in the art world. It's also why I got a bit into technology."

She also thickened her liberal arts portfolio. In addition to co-writing the book "Water: More or Less" with Rita Schmidt Sudman, Taylor has been writing and illustrating semiregular pieces for the Sacramento Bee's Forum section, "California Sketches," which provides her the chance to "be a political philosopher and comment on cause and effect." She also recently illustrated the Sacramento Library's new edition of Mary Shelley's classic "Frankenstein.

Taylor holds a bachelor's degree from UCLA in history — not, as one might suspect, in art, though she realizes she might have been hardwired for the latter. "I just know I always drew," she recalls, "and I was always a problem solver. I hope it's not my memory rewriting the narrative. All I know is when I was 5 years old, I wanted to draw my mom walking up a staircase in profile. But the perspective was all off, and I figured out the only way to make it look realistic was to have the risers all be different heights." She offers that crooked smile of hers. "I guess there are engineering and architecture genes in here as well as art ones," she says.

Her late mom, Theo Samuels, was "an artist and actually, a damn good painter." Her dad, George, had a career in wholesale. "They each made it to the age of 94 1/2," Taylor says, though her father died years before her mother. Taylor has three grown children and four grandchildren "so far. Two more are in the oven." Her daughter is expecting twins.

Currently, Taylor is working on a commission for Otto Construction: a 7-foot tall, 10-foot wide acrylic painting of construction workers. She's also been commissioned to do a series of life-size crow sculptures — her drawings have been making the rounds on Facebook — and an outdoor fountain for Lyon Real Estate. She's also occasionally rehired by clients to freshen or fix one of her works that's been battered by the elements or less-than-gracefully handled relocations.

Asked to tersely characterize herself, Taylor says, "I'm a maker. A worker bee. I want to do transformative pieces, not decorative ones. After 50 years, I still think of myself as pushing the boundaries, maybe even my own."

Catherine Kleckner checks one off her bucket list

C atherine Kleckner got the key to the first art gallery she's ever owned on Oct. 1, 2017. By Nov. 2, she was able to hold the grand opening of CK Art, having spent the previous four weeks turning a former Birkenstock footwear store in midtown Sacramento into a showplace that wouldn't be out of place in lower Manhattan's SoHo district.

"It really wasn't that hard," she says in the high-pitched, eager voice that belies her 35 years and considerable experience in the art world. "It mainly involved taking down all the shoe shelves, painting all of the walls white and redoing the backroom floor." That room used to hold the store's inventory of built-for-comfort sandals and shoes. It's now an additional exhibit space, allowing two shows to be up at the same time.

For example, starting April 1, the front room of the gallery, which faces J and 25th streets, will be a multiple-artist show under the rubric, "Welcome to the Flower Shop." The back room will feature a solo exhibit of new works by Tyson Anthony Roberts, who says his pieces are inspired by urban and rural landscapes but are more expressionistic and abstract than what you might expect. (I like them a lot, have never met the artist, am a fairly serious art collector and don't have a stake in the gallery. So there.)

"Owning a gallery was always on my bucket list," Kleckner says, sitting in the big, airy, front room and listening to cars swish by. It had rained all morning and the sun was now playing peek-a-boo with the mashed-potato clouds. It was a perfect time to be sitting in a calm space looking at beautiful things.

"I always thought this was something I'd do when I was closer to retirement. But I fell in love with this space — the windows, the light, being able to watch people go by and drop in to visit," she says. "I've met all the business owners around me and the other gallery owners, who've been surprisingly supportive."

Kleckner says she was surprised because in her years as an art consultant — the person companies and institutions hire to advise them on what to buy for their environments to enhance the experience for customers and their own staff — she "found a lot of the gallery owners to be very competitive. Now, we're all in the same boat. We'd like to see midtown continue to be a center for arts activities."

In fact, at almost the same coordinates as her gallery — 25th and J streets — is the new Groundswell gallery, co-founded by popular local artist Micah Crandall-Bear, photographer John Johnson of Seattle and Jaime Caluya.

Unlike many galleries whose owners don't think of Second Saturday as playing a major role in immediate sales, Kleckner said that for her, the monthly art tour/pub crawl has been "the biggest traffic generator and resulted in a lot of my sales." Even so — again, like many other owners — she hosts an artist reception on the Thursday evening prior to Second Saturday.

While Kleckner claims not to be an artist herself, she certainly spent years educating her eyes. Her college years at Sonoma State University, where she earned her bachelor's degree, included a year of study at California State University's international program in Florence — yes, that Florence, the one they keep in Italy — followed by earning her master's degree in contemporary art from Sotheby's Institute of Art in New York City. Among her other adventures were three years working with highly regarded art consultant Kira Stewart.

I ask her if she foresees a time when sitting alone in a gallery if customers don't arrive in droves that day may wear her down. "It's been a whirlwind of a few months," she says, "and all I know is that when I unlock the door each morning, I feel positively giddy."

April 25, 2018

Classical soprano Carrie Hennessey sings for Sacramento music lovers

" **I** feel like I was born in the wrong era," says Carrie Hennessey, a globally respected lyric soprano who happens to live in North Natomas. "The 1950s and '60s were the golden age of classical singing. Today, there's less focus on the voice. But I work pretty steadily."

No kidding. In the past few years, Hennessey has played, among other top roles, Blanche DuBois ("I have always depended on the kindness of strangers") in the operatic version of Tennessee Williams' "A Streetcar Named Desire," earning raves in, among other media outlets, the Fresno Bee. Its critic wrote that the singer "gave us a Blanche that let us burrow into her character's soul, even into the darkest crevices. ...Hennessey, using a one-two punch of music and drama, made it resonate in a way that equaled the finest stage performances of the part I've seen."

If you caught her in the Sacramento Ballet's recent staging of "Carmina Burana," you heard and saw her sing as a member of the chorus but also in a number of solos, which received applause as loud as that for the dancers. She's also played one of my favorite roles, Mimi, in "La Bohéme," which prompted the San Francisco Classical Voice to laud her "exquisite vocal purity and range," adding that Hennessey was "nothing short of sensational."

Hennessey is 44, the mother of two and the eighth child of her parents, though she was born a full decade after the seventh. It meant that, growing up, "I was (all of my nieces' and nephews') aunt, big sister, chauffer, coach and confidante." She laughs — a sound as marvelously robust and clear as her singing voice — and says, "My mother used to say, 'Music and humor will get you through anything.' "

In fact, her late mom, Dorothy Rosquist, became Hennessey's first musical accompanist. But even before that, when Hennessey was a baby and her mother was the church pianist in their Minneapolis neighborhood church, "My mom used to pedal the piano with one foot and rock my cradle with the other."

I ask Hennessey about her early musical influences and she rapidly replies, "Growing up in Minnesota and listening to the New York Metropolitan Opera performing live on the radio gave me a sort of homey feel." She clasps her hands to her face and says, "Believe me, I've tried to think of another word to describe it, but 'homey' keeps winning."

She did a regional audition for the Met some years back and it resulted in her walking away from opera and singing altogether for a full 12 years. "I was singing just fine and all of a sudden my voice cracked slightly. Well, for me, that was it. I grabbed my music and walked out before they could tell me to."

Hennessey says it's only "in the last few months" that she's discovered "I'm finally comfortable in my skin as a singer." It didn't prevent her from maintaining an active performance schedule but she says she finally got to the point where "it all made sense. This is what I was born to do."

On stage, Hennessey is a commanding presence. Sloe-eyed and radiant, she's as much of an actress as a singer — which is not to diminish the capacity of her voice, which she nevertheless downplays. "I have a big enough lyric (soprano) but it's not a dominant one."

Over time, Hennessey and her husband of nearly 20 years, Patrick, gravitated from holding serious jobs — he in information technology, she in banking — to becoming members of the gig economy. In other words, they make their own work. Patrick's a drummer in "an Irish punk band called Pikeys," his wife says proudly. Hennessey herself isn't always submerged in the classical life: She has her own "mash-up band" (it does a little bit of everything) called The ReAssemblers of Whimsy.

You can learn more about Hennessey on her website or better yet, catch her live, this Sunday at 3 p.m., performing with pianist Jason Sherbundy in a show they're calling "To Live and Die for Love: The Heroines of Puccini." It's being held at Pioneer United Methodist Church in Auburn as a benefit for the Auburn Interfaith Food Closet's new building fund.

I'll be there — and if you are, too, I think you'll agree we're very lucky she was born in this era.

First a gallery, then a wedding: Meet two co-founders of Groundswell

T his past Valentine's Day, four days after opening Groundswell, their first art gallery, Jaime (pronounced Jamey) Caluya and John Johnson embarked on another joint venture: They got married in San Francisco and flew off to honeymoon in Key West.

Caluya is a pharmacist, real estate investor and classically trained pianist (though she admits to being "shy" about the latter). She lived much of her life in Australia. Johnson, a musician, photographer and video producer, has roots here but had been living in Seattle. They first saw each other at a watering hole "meet-up" that Caluya had organized, where Johnson was playing bass in the band. Thereafter began a cross-continental romance, which, I'm guessing, tested the limits of frequent-flyer miles.

Joining them last Wednesday afternoon for a cocktail at Wildwood in Pavilions Shopping Center, I find myself almost as smitten with the couple as they are with each other. I resist the urge to pronounce them "adorable" but that's the word that keeps crowding my mind as I watch them interact.

I notice that each wears a wedding ring on the right hand. "Well, I'm mainly left-handed, you see, so I'd be constantly slamming it if it were on that hand," says Caluya, a native of the Philippines with a melodic Australian accent and semi-formal speaking style.

"And on my left hand, it would get in the way when I play guitar," Johnson says. This exchange is apparently enough for the two to exchange looks, then enlace their hands and arms around each other. The word "beaming" may have been invented to describe this couple. (I remind myself to look away: I may be pre-diabetic.)

But don't kid yourself: These two are serious about their new business. Groundswell is an airy gallery on J Street, just a few doors east of 25th Street in midtown Sacramento — and just a building or so away from CK Art Gallery, another new space I wrote about a few weeks back. The market for art appears to be making a comeback in Sacramento.

When they took over their space, which had been occupied for many years by Art Ellis art supply store and then by other retailer, "It was basically destroyed," Johnson says. "I mean, there were dead rats. I went there every day, with contractors and carpenters but was also doing a lot of the cleanup myself." He pauses and seems to remember he left something out. "As was Jaime," he adds thoughtfully, which makes both of them laugh.

Micah Crandall-Bear, a talented and increasingly ubiquitous artist whose work has been bursting out of Sacramento, is a co-owner of Groundswell but spends most of his time pursuing his art career, Johnson says. He adds, "But I think it's worth noting that the name for the gallery came from the title of a multimedia piece he and I had been collaborating on," featuring photography and painting.

Johnson is 48, Caluya 41. They both look much younger — being in love and on dual journeys together, romance and business, probably doesn't hurt. I ask who makes such seemingly routine but necessary decisions like which painting will hang there and which sculpture will be stood here. "Well," Johnson begins, "I'm the allegedly creative one and Jaime is horrifically organized" — Caluya laughs at that — "so you'd think I'd be the one hanging the art. But..."

"I have definite ideas about which pieces should go where," Caluya gently cuts in. "I have to keep reminding myself that I began my studies in the sciences as well as painting."

"So when we disagree, we solve it by one of us saying, 'Okay,' " Johnson says. He laughs and adds, "Usually me."

Nanami Cowdroy's drawings and Akira Beard's painting and illustrations will be exhibited in May. Details are at the gallery's website, which features music and videos. I'm not sure if Caluya or Johnson is deciding on placement of the pieces. But I'm pretty sure this marriage will last.

May 10, 2018

Sisters start Forever Glass to give work and meaning to autism patients

Today is Mother's Day in Mexico so this column may be too late to help you if that's the one you observe. If, on the other hand, you're looking for a gift that's unique, handcrafted, transparent and memorable, may I suggest you go bowling.

Actually, the keepsake recycled-glass bowls created by Forever Glass, a family company housed on a 48-acre ranch in the woody, air-conditioned hills just above Placerville, won't be ready for you to present on American Mother's day, which I've heard from reliable sources is Sunday.

But you can still go online, select and order a bowl and get a gift card to present from foreverglass.works (definitely one of the more cleverly named URLs out there). You'll not only be making a mom smile — you'll be helping give meaningful work to young artisans who are on what's called the "autistic spectrum" and/or are developmentally disabled. Like Cathy Porter's 30-year-old son, Richard.

"We started this in 2016," says Porter, who co-founded Forever Glass with her sister, Bernadette Guimarin, a retired U. S. Air Force veteran. "We realized we were nearly out of our fabulous 50s" — Porter is 59, Guimarin 57 — "and I wanted to make sure my son, and others on the spectrum, would have a good way to make a living when my husband James and I aren't around anymore."

The bowls are "spun," a rare glass-art process that repurposes pieces of buyers' memorabilia — a glass goblet or wine bottle from a wedding or birthday, for example — which, with other glass chunks, are mashed and hashed in

71

a firing oven at 2,250 degrees Fahrenheit. When they reach that temperature, which you really can say is hotter than hell, they're molded into the new bowls. All of them sell for $99, Porter says, though they do charge an extra $25 for engraving.

In fact, if you order at the speed of light, you may still be able to buy a bowl that was signed by Temple Grandin, the world-renowned professor of animal science at Colorado State University who is herself on the autism spectrum. I wrote about Grandin on March 26 and went to hear her speak one chilly evening at the end of April at the Shingle Springs ranch of Dr. Steve and Beverly Barad. I was one of more than 600 attendees, many of whom were horse breeders and horse lovers, who turned out to hear Grandin talk about caring for animals but also about autism. She was wonderful: witty, wise and intense. She sets an example for others who've been diagnosed with autism — but more to the point, she singlehandedly evaporates stereotypes about the word, which sets an example for the rest of us.

So check out that website. Who says you can only have a super bowl in winter?

Art consultant Kira Stewart expands her brand

Kira Stewart — the city-trotting, increasingly in-demand art consultant, mostly to the health care industry — says she loves surprises. And the best ones come from those for whom she helps create comforting environments.

Even though hospitals, clinics and social-service practitioners hire her and her firm, Art Consulting Services, Stewart sees her ultimate clients as the children being cared for in pediatric oncology units and the frail, low-income adults in special-care centers like Sutter Health's new PACE program — people who have their own opinions of the sort of paintings, photos and sculptures that will lighten their moods when physical or emotional duress are routinely on the agenda.

Those opinions are what sometimes surprise her — because they can differ from those of the professionals who have, in good faith, made certain presumptions. These could include a belief that most kids will love pictures of baby animals, and most seniors will love homily-filled wall hangings that may have been considered kitschy even in their own time period. Stewart listens carefully to the opinions of the specialists — then, working with them, helps organize focus groups in which the patients offer their own views.

"Eighty percent of our design and art consulting is in the health care field," Stewart says one recent, very warm afternoon in her East Sacramento office, a modest second-floor one-time apartment entered separately from the home below. The workplace, which houses Stewart's all-female staff of four full- and two part-time employees, is a testament to the kind of work ACS does for clients in 17 different cities (and counting): colorful and art-filled but far from fussy. The words that quickly come to mind are "upbeat" and "engaging."

Those words also could be used to characterize Stewart, who's celebrating the 12th anniversary of her company this month— and, as you read this, is on an African safari (but checking emails, of course). "We just passed the 500-projects mark," she announces without the slightest pretense of being blasé about it. "We're doing 30 to 75 projects a year, all over the state."

And while the company retains the name and logo it's always had, Stewart has given it a new tagline ("When art is more than art") to reflect the additional work she and her staff do to make certain that each project is about more than selecting art and other visuals for each facility's décor.

"Our work used to be about just finding the right 'vibe' for a place," she says, "and it almost became a checklist approach. But our focus now is to make much more of an impact." And, as aforementioned, that focus involves focus groups. She organized a committee of 10-year-olds at a pediatric clinic and showed them some animal photos and paintings. They told her in no uncertain terms that they didn't like what they saw. "One of the kids said, 'I feel like the animals are looking at me and it scares me.' When it's late, and their moms and dads go home, and you're awake and feel like you're all alone in the world, that can be pretty upsetting."

Sometimes Stewart and her designers walk into an aesthetically neglected clinic and end up "starting from ground zero. I mean, some of these places look like the paintings were bought at a garage sale. The interior may have five different styles of molding. We've found that by creating new environments, it not only cheers the patients but also the staffs. They're suddenly proud of the place they work. They bring their own families to take tours."

One bit of research that Stewart shares during our chat is especially eye-opening. "People think if there are more floors in a building, they'll get better care there," she says. I guess when it comes to the mystery of medicine, there are plenty of tall stories.

A CAPITAL LIFE

Sacramento is a star of 'Lady Bird'

So we went to see "Lady Bird," Sacramento native Greta Gerwig's absolutely charming coming-of-age movie, at the Tower Theatre late the other afternoon. I urge anyone who grew up here, used to live here or currently lives here to go see this film, which I'm guessing is going to be up for some major awards, including an Oscar nod for Gerwig's screenplay. The talented cast includes Sacramento itself and, not to be a name-dropper, my car.

Seriously. In a scene that apparently was filmed from the front lawn of my former house on 40th Street (I know because it's a shot of people coming out of Burnett and Mimi Miller's home, just across the street from mine), there's a two-shot of the main character, Christine, who calls herself Lady Bird, and her mother sitting in their car together. Behind them, parked at the curb and slightly out-of-focus, is my 15-year-old silver-gray Mercedes E-320. I'm guessing that at the time of the shoot, it was more like 13 years old.

Throughout the film, the audience at the Tower Theatre chattered and laughed appreciatively. The Tower was shown in the movie, making the viewing experience slightly surrealistic. I think some of us expected the camera to suddenly zoom indoors and find us there watching the film we would now be in. (Well, maybe just a few of us expected that. Maybe just me. I have to cut down on the Advil).

There were shots of people driving on the J Street bridge over the American River, of various stores and schools, even of the U.S. Post Office on 48th and J Streets, where my date and I had dropped off some mail on the way to the show. (And no, we weren't seen in the film doing so. I mean, come on, that would be silly.)

Ed Goldman: Don't Cry For Me, Ardent Reader

In a scene in the movie during which high school kids rehearse a musical, Erik Daniells, the young man who played the piano at my daughter's wedding in my backyard in 2011, can be seen. So can some other young Sacramentans, some of whom I recognized from the local drama scene.

Saoirse Ronan, the young woman who plays the title role, is quite reminiscent of writer-director Gerwig, a fine actress whose talk-show appearances show her to be as quick-witted as the character based on her — and just as adorably goofy. Lady Bird's mother in the film is played by stage actress Laurie Metcalf, who I think will also nab an Oscar nomination, for supporting actress. The father is acted by Tracy Letts, a great playwright/actor; he goes so deep into a role that I didn't recognize him. He won the 2008 Pulitzer Prize for writing the play, "August: Osage County," and a Tony Award for playing George in "Who's Afraid of Virginia Woolf?" You also may know his face if you're a fan of cable-TV's "Homeland," in which he played Andrew Lockhart.

Sacramento is filmed with great care, beauty and a sense of nostalgia. Though the film is set only 15 years ago, that can comprise an eternity in a young person's life. The film made me a little sentimental, too — especially when I saw that shot of my car. I mean, in 2002, it was brand new.

A napping class at UC Davis is something to sleep through

N apping is now a part of the curriculum at University of California Davis — not just a byproduct of the curriculum at UC Davis.

In response to a number of studies that indicate students are working just too doggone hard (poor babies) the campus is offering a class in, essentially, how to nap.

This is all according to a recent Capital Public Radio report by Sammy Caiola, a fine reporter who used to cover health stories for the Sacramento Bee. (The Bee wrote about it a few days later, too. I'm sure it was just a coincidence. Absolutely sure.)

"This quarter," Caiola reported, "a noncredit 30-minute power-nap class gives students a quiet place to snooze. They curl up in thick blankets and lay down on yoga mats, using eye masks to block out the midday sun. An instructor guides them in meditation."

She adds: "U.S. college students get roughly seven hours of sleep each night, but experts say they really need nine to function well."

Nine? That's what I got every two nights when I was that age.

Now, I confess that when I was a college student, I occasionally fell asleep in early-morning classes (I never did this as a college instructor, you'll be pleased, and possibly surprised, to learn). I worked a late shift at a newspaper, from roughly 3 p.m. to midnight, and when I left work, was too wired to go right home to bed, much less to sleep once I got there. I was 19 and found every day and night at the newspaper beyond stimulating. (I added that last part to get a laugh from everyone in the Business Journal newsroom. And maybe even the Bee's.)

The few times I conked out in class, I awoke myself almost immediately because I thought I heard someone, far, far away, snoring. Alas, it was me. I'm sure I only compounded the comedy (and my embarrassment) by snapping to so abruptly and clumsily that I knocked everything off my desk and lap, including books, papers and very strong (though obviously ineffective) coffee. If anyone had wondered who'd been snoring, my slapstick actions clarified it.

"The school also provides a 'nap map' of sleepable couches, grass lawns and hammocks around campus," Caiola said. So this is what it's come to: GPS now means global positioning snoozes. Enroll me!

That Fab 40s house listing for $3.9 million? No!

I don't usually regret things in life even though there are many things I should. Oh, I'll feel bad about something I said, and I'll have no qualms about apologizing. But I guess I learned at a very young age that "regret" almost always refers to something that happened already and I can't undo.

An exception to this is when I send "regrets" that I won't be attending an event I wouldn't have gone to in the first place, not even if they'd promised to hand me crispy thousand-dollar bills upon my arrival. In this usage, I'm regretting something in the future. But I'm really not. So when I juice it up by writing to the inviter, "I sincerely regret I can't make it," I'm lying twice: with the adverb "sincerely" and the verb "regret."

That said, when I read this week that one of the Fab 40s homes shown in "Lady Bird" — the greatest (and only) film ever made about growing up awkward in East Sacramento — went on the market for $3.9 million, I experienced first a pang, then a throbbing, then what I thought might be a minor stroke. In short, I felt a deep sense of regret that I'd sold my own Fab 40s home before the film was released and all the hoopla surrounding it commenced.

To be clear about this, my home wasn't shown in "Lady Bird." But as I pointed out in my column of Nov. 28, 2017, my car was. It was sitting in front of my home in a short scene when the title character and her mom were arguing (I know what you're thinking: pick a scene in which they weren't arguing). I've deduced that part of that scene, which included a shot of my neighbor's home across the street, would have to have been shot while the cinematographer stood in my front yard. Doesn't that count for something? If it had been your home, wouldn't you have capitalized on its just-off-screen, cameo nonappearance?

But, alas, by the time the film came out, it already had been a year since I sold my place (on Thanksgiving Day 2016, to be exact). I had neither asked nor received $3.9 million for it. I certainly didn't do badly on the deal but at that time, the home's only known claim to fame was that my daughter had been married in its backyard in 2011 and that John Travolta had walked by it while taking a break from shooting, a block or two away, the misnamed film "Lucky Numbers" (it was a box office disaster).

So here's what I intend to do: contact a few Hollywood car collectors and see if any of them would like to buy my car for only, say, $3.8 million (after all, a car is not a home). I know I'd miss driving it. But I definitely wouldn't have any regrets.

A handy guide for Bay Area expats

Wanting to "get out of Dodge" is a common desire. But when Dodge is San Francisco — and as many as 46 percent of its denizens say they plan to abandon the city-by-the-bay in the next few years — that's quite another.

When you factor in that as many as 5 percent of these wannabe expats may migrate to Sacramento, according to a number of reports, well, trend-watchers, we now have a full-blown, bona-fide Thing.

Concerned, I called my always-reluctant re-lo adviser, Knott Goen, to ask him some questions about the looming migration. An excerpt of our three-and-a-half-hour conversation (we were driving to San Francisco on a Friday) follows.

Q: Where will we put that many newcomers?

A: Well, I suggest stuffing them all into a handful of aging, two-room/one-bath apartment houses in the noisiest part of the city, at least 45 minutes from their jobs. That last part will ease the transition for them. Sudden change can prove to be a shock to the system, as you know. Just ask the millions of us who began drinking heavily in November 2016.

Q: What will the emigrants do with the spare time they accrue from not having twice-daily two-hour commutes?

A: Many of them will begin drinking heavily. No, just kidding. I think those who survive the constant hitting of themselves up the side of the head while yelling,

"Why didn't I do this years ago?" will slowly find out that Sacramento has a number of professional and semiprofessional theaters, dance companies, orchestras, art galleries, first-class restaurants, professional sports, athletic clubs and, most important of all to feel at home, elitist snobs.

Q: Why is that last part important?

A: Well, think of how many people who live in San Francisco call it "The City," as opposed to "a city." Or who lump the entire region into something called "The Barria."

Q: What's "The Barria?"

A: "The Bay Area" when you say it without moving your teeth. We need to learn how to do that here. It's too bad Thurston Howell III of "Gilligan's Island" is dead. He could have taught us.

Q: It's certainly worth discuss —

A: "CruhMENto." How do you like it?

Q: Not a whole lot.

A: Almost sounds like "pimento," doesn't it? I'd try garbling "Farm to Fork" in the same way but I'm sure it'd come out sounding profane.

Aug. 3, 2018

Six reasons I'll never fit in, in Sacramento

I moved to Sacramento in the late summer of 1976. In some towns and cultures, that'd make you all but a native. Not here. And here's a list of six reasons why I know, in my heart or hearts, I'll never fit in.

1. I'll never get laryngitis shouting my encouragement at a Kings game. I'd rather get it attempting to imitate Tony Bennett belting out "I Left My Heart In San Francisco" while washing my hair in the shower. My reasoning is that while both activities are futile and both leave you feeling hoarse, only one leaves you in dismay.

2. I don't join the standing ovations at the conclusion of every single ballet, philharmonic, theater and concert event in town. The two exceptions occur when what I've seen has gone far beyond the expected (after all, these people are professionals — why shouldn't they have delivered?) and also when, having sat in discomfort for two hours or more, I need to stretch my back or rearrange my undershorts.

3. If I have an emceeing gig, I'll rarely introduce an elected Sacramento official as "the honorable" anything. That's not because I don't respect a number of them. It just seems like a hollow compliment — unless we start directing it to everyone we feel has behaved well: "I'd like you to meet the honorable Brad Wallrich, the HVAC expert

at Garick, who didn't charge me for a house call when all I needed to do was turn the air conditioner on to make it work." "This is the honorable Robert Harris, the attorney who told me at brunch, and without charging me thereafter, that I didn't really need to establish an LLC to sell my ocarina on eBay."

4. I'll never take the tour at Sutter's Fort. Oh, I'm sure the docents are terrific. But if I can't find my own way through a place that small without a human GPS to guide me, I have some serious orientation challenges I'd best discuss with the honorable Dana Hawkins, my family doctor. (Note: These are all real names.)

5. I will never attend the annual farm-to-fork Tower Bridge dinner unless invited by a time traveler — the only one who could bag a seat since when tickets go on sale, they disappear in minus10 seconds. In the spirit of same, however, I plan to spend that day sitting in direct sunlight in my backyard eating a salad of my locally sourced clover weeds.

6. I will never praise the exterior design of the Mondavi Center. The indoor design and acoustics, you bet. But from the freeway, the building looks like cardboard file boxes, the kind you see disgraced executives carrying to their cars as they're being escorted from the building. Note to architecture fans: Yes, I know the box design enhances the sound, and I love attending events at the Mondavi. Truth be told, sometimes when I'm there, I even join the standing ovations — if Tony Bennett has just performed.

YOUR GOVERNMENT INACTION

Who did the metrics on new parking fees?

As soon as someone says "metrics" in a conversation, I glaze over faster than a honey-baked ham.

People use the word to mean a variety of things, just as they often do with "marketing" (sales? public relations? research?). The website Investopedia (yes, it exists) defines metrics as "parameters or measures of quantitative assessment used for measurement, comparison or to track performance or production."

Let's translate that from its original Esperanto: You use metrics to compare stuff. And I'm hoping that the city of Sacramento considered some serious metrics before adopting its new business model for downtown parking (code name: Wild in the Streets).

The basic comparison for me would be this:

Will people in the suburbs, who rarely flocked to downtown Sacramento before, now do so in spite of higher, frequently baffling parking fees — fees that are needed to pay for the Golden 1 Center, which is the main reason people are flocking downtown? ("It would be an absolute honor for me to pay more money to park near an arena that will charge me to patronize it!")

Analysts can point to San Francisco — where you can get slapped with a pricey ticket while you're still in the actual process of parking, or so it seems — and say, "Look: People still go there to shop, watch plays, eat in restaurants and stay in the hotels (which also charge you to park there). So what's the problem?"

Well, downtown Sacramento, as much as I love it, is not downtown San Francisco. You don't skip a trip to San Francisco because there are plenty of other restaurants and stores in Millbrae. San Francisco is a destination because it's an environment, a state of mind, a way of life.

Sacramento is getting there, too. But if you live in Sacramento's suburbs, you can find just as many theaters (the Harris Center in Folsom, to name just three), stores and good restaurants without having to pay a dime for parking.

You don't need a special app to tell you when your meter's expiring because there aren't any meters. And there are plenty of hotels there, which also don't charge you to park your car.

My point is that if we blow this opportunity to become truly metropolitan by shutting out the very people who can help get us there, there won't be any coming back, even if the Kings start winning and five new restaurants open. We won't need metrics to figure that out.

A bogus robocall from the IRS can be taxing

So I get one of those bogus IRS robocalls the other day — you know the one, in which a harsh, disappointed-in-you female voice says your property and life are being monitored by the IRS prior to your being arrested. I'm surprised the voice doesn't add, "Oh, and have a nice day."

So I start to dial the callback number just for fun (well, really so I can get a column out of it. I never could fool you). The area code is 253, which is my first surprise: Shouldn't the IRS at least give you a toll-free number to call prior to arresting you? It would leave a better taste in your mouth, don't you agree?

So I look online to see where that area code emanates from and get a brief shock when I see it's Washington. Then I exhale and realize it's for the state of Washington, not Washington, D.C. I ask myself: Has the IRS moved its headquarters to Seattle/Tacoma/Puget Sound? Does it throw tax scofflaws from the top of the Space Needle as a lesson to the rest of us?

So then I'm reminded of what my accountant told me the last time I received a few of these calls. "They're fake," he said, "and you'd think the IRS would want to crack down on them."

So then I get angry. Most of us, at anytime in our work and personal lives, are involved in some sort of financial transactions. In my case, the call comes as I'm signing papers at two title companies — one for the sale of my home and one for the purchase of my new one. There have been complications (truly not my doing), and the deal has been dragging. Lenders, escrow officers and title company people have been a bit up in arms about one of the players (truly not me).

We're dealing with government entities. How do we know that something hasn't aroused the interest of the actual IRS?

So I try to replay the voicemail I received, but I apparently had deleted it. I want to call that 253 number and go through the whole sordid, crooked call with them until they ask (as they inevitably will) for my Social Security number. I'll tape the call. I'll turn the tape over to the real IRS. It'll send me a lovely gift.

So then I remember that the best strategy for most of us is to not deal personally with the IRS. That's why we hire CPAs. Hence, even while attempting to do something good, I may do myself some harm.

So I head downstairs, mix a martini and flip on "Jeopardy." And, at last, I start to have that nice day.

Has the U.S. Postal Service gone commercial?

I'll bet you didn't know that when you change your address with the U.S. Postal Service, you also can do the following:

- Save 20 percent on "items for your new home" at Kohl's.

- Get 20 percent off on one-day rentals with Budget.

- Buy $100,000 of life insurance from Globe Life and Accident Insurance Co. — where "all calls (are) proudly serviced in the USA" — for as little as $3.49 per month for adults and $2.17 per month for children and grandchildren.

- Get a Visa credit card from State Farm with a "zero percent APR on purchases and balance transfers through 12 billing cycles."

If this sounds to you like one of those old late-night TV spots for Veg-O-Matic — or a current one on the Home Shopping Network — come sit beside me. Something's changed with our beloved ol' USPS. This isn't your father's post office, kids. It doesn't even sound like it's your Uncle Sam's.

Well, rest assured that the USPS is still a federal operation. Contrary to rumor, it's become neither a private business nor a "quasi-governmental entity" as some people believe. (It's undoubtedly still a nonprofit, though probably not by intent.)

I see how we can be confused. The first clue, I suppose, is discovering that the post office's website is usps.com

— not usps.gov or even usps.org. With all of the product placement in the change-of-address package, I'm surprised it's not usps.biz.

The post office's products used to be just those: products branded by the post office. You could buy envelopes, packing tape and festive stamps at the counter. You can still do that, of course. But now, the office has adopted a mercantile vibe, targeting and partnering with businesses whose services or products may come to mind when, as in my case, you're about to move.

We mustn't blame the gang at the post office for this sea change.

About 46 years ago, the Postal Reorganization Act came into being with the intent of making the post office a kind of enterprise fund — which is to say, financed by its own revenue. So you have to applaud it for trying to operate in a more businesslike way, with promotional tie-ins and so forth.

Accordingly, I'd like to propose two other possible revenue sources:

1. Offer naming rights to local offices, charging well-heeled companies and individuals the chance to enhance their brands. Naturally, there'd have to be certain controls put in place: No one is really ready for a Midas Muffler or Hooters branch office.

2. Create an adopt-a-mail-carrier program. This would help the Postal Service keep pace with its employees' salary and benefits packages. And if you found you didn't like the mail person you adopted, the solution would be simple: Hang a sign around his or her neck that says, "Return to Sender."

March 27, 2017

A bill for zero? From City Hall?

T he utility service division at the city of Sacramento thrilled me beyond words the other day. It sent me a bill for $0.00.

I think this had to do with my having canceled one water/trash/gutter account and starting another, because of my move from East Sacramento to what I'm calling Easter Sacramento. Things happened so quickly and overlapped so messily that it must have confused the system, since my bill arrived with a payment envelope.

That part made me laugh and I fought the urge to write out a check — with a fountain pen, in elaborate cursive and a memo at the bottom, "for municipal services rendered."

It got me to thinking how easy it would be for other government agencies to put some sparkle in our day simply by sending us nice little notes.

1. From the IRS — Dear Taxpayer: You know, we've been looking at your payment record over a 20-year period and must admit we've marveled at your punctuality, honesty and timeliness. Since we're not really sure where your tax dollars go — one guy here did but he retired a few months ago and it's been guesswork ever since — we've unanimously decided to have you forego paying us anything for calendar year 2016. And if we actually owe you anything, we'd appreciate you applying the same courtesy to us. (Ha, ha. LOL. We'll refund whatever we owe you, Pal. We just enjoy a good chuckle now and then here at your Department of the Treasury.)

2. From the Department of Immigration — Dear Melting Potters: Hey, the foreign-travel ban is over; we're not shipping your spouses, siblings and house pets back to your country of origin and we're sooooo sorry for the inconvenience, ulcers and tears. Seems we made a big booboo in our calculations, finally realizing that if we got rid of all U.S. immigrants, there'd be a maximum of 473 people left in the country. We don't think this is what we had in mind when we started downsizing. In any event, please forgive the tsooris, as our good friends the Israelis say.

3. From the Department of Motor Vehicles — Dear Texting Teenage Driver: Is our face red! Had we known you were texting your BFF to say you were running a little late but that you'd managed to speed through every light after it turned red, we're sure to have dismissed the $450 ticket we issued you (the one that had the photo of you nearly knocking down the elderly couple in the crosswalk). Look, we may be the DMV, but we're also parents. We know how important your cyber life is as you develop into a contributing member of society. Let's say no more about the ticket. Rest assured, the officer who stopped you, put you in handcuffs and hauled you in — because of your expired license, no proof of insurance and the naughty name you called him — has been disciplined. But in the future, please remember: If you can't say something nice to someone, do what our president does: Send the person a tweet. Some people find this highly irritating but listen, how else will we make America grate again.

Tips for NASA's plan to send a rocket to the sun

As you might have heard, NASA plans to send a rocket to the sun as early as next year. And while the rocket isn't supposed to get any closer than 4 million miles from its destination, I still think NASA should charge the trip to its American Express card — because even if the rocket flies only about 88 million miles, it should easily qualify for mileage bonus points.

In an effort to establish my creds as a long-range thinker, here are some other tips for the gang at NASA.

1. Don't call this Project Icarus. Icarus is the guy in Greek mythology who ignored his father's instructions and flew too close to the sun, which melted the wings his dad had developed for him, leaving us with the most overused metaphor in the history of humankind about overreaching. It was also what the main villain called his world-domination device in the last James Bond film to star Pierce Brosnan. So, all in all, the name can't portend good things.

2. Go at night. This is an old joke, I realize, but an old joke often contains wisdom. Not this old joke, necessarily. But still.

3. Though it may seem counterintuitive, don't rely on solar power. Bring along an emergency generator.

4. Slather the rocket with lotion containing an SPF count of at least 175,000. Avoid cocoa butter at all costs.

5. Put a light-colored sheath on the rocket, which will deflect the sun's rays. This is why people who wear white swimsuits to the beach never ever burn.

6. For extra protection, strap former celebrity George Hamilton and former Congressman John Boehner to the rocket. Their deep, metallic bronze complexions should absorb a high percentage of the sun's rays while, for them, it'll just be like adding an extra layer of tan, an always welcome plus at the country club.

7. If the rocket will be refueled in space, don't let it take a refreshing dip in a Martian canal for at least two hours afterward.

8. Don't tie any sandwiches with mayonnaise to the rocket. Especially not an egg salad sandwich. That's just asking for trouble.

9. If the rocket actually makes it back to earth, have plenty of aloe vera or Vaseline Petroleum Jelly ready to smooth on it. Don't look alarmed if in a day or two its veneer starts to peel.

10. Don't take it out on the rocket when you look at the photos it shot and find all of them to be over-exposed. What did you expect, folks? Always try to have the sun behind you when you take snaps. How'd you get such good grades in science class, anyway?

Privatizing government?
I have some ideas

As the Sacramento City Council looks into privatizing operations of the convention center complex, I've begun to wonder what other government entities could benefit from private-sector engagement.

A brief list follows.

1. The U.S. Congress: Let's face a hard fact. Neither the Senate nor House of Representatives can be said to run like a fine Swiss watch. A fine Swiss cheese may be a closer analogy, with its imperfect symmetry, irregular holes and slightly acrid aftertaste. My suggestion: Run Congress like Major League Baseball. Junior senators and junior congresspersons would be the minor league team, senior elected officials would be major league players, the president would be the general manager and his cabinet would become the team owners. Their first job would be to fire the GM. Ah, what dreams will come.

2. The Transportation Safety Administration: You know who'd be much better at doing body searches for weaponry? The Mafia. Its members are also a little more intimidating than the TSA airport workers (with a few notable exceptions. I still feel a little bad for the aggressive guy who demanded to inspect the colostomy bag I wore for a few months about 10 years ago). My thought is that if you had a guy on the other side of the X-ray machine who went by the name of Frankie Hot Pockets, Ziggy Ginsu or Nicky Nitro, nobody would try to smuggle contraband

shampoo or Cuban cigars onto a plane.

3. U.S. Embassies: This is a prime opportunity for Nordstrom, the company that made courtesy and problem-solving a core value. If a Nordstrom clothing salesperson can make you feel terrific about yourself in a new outfit you'd have never dared considering, think what that salesperson could accomplish if brought in to negotiate the Israeli-Palestinian conflict. Peace in the region at last? Oh, darling, it's you!

4. City councils themselves: Elected and appointed officials at the Southern California city of Bell ran their town like a business and it worked out great — for a while, anyway. The problem was that they weren't really businesspeople. They were bureaucrats and local politicians who thought they were acting like businesspeople. Unfortunately, their role models were the villains in Frank Capra movies and the real-life Bernie Madoff, as portrayed in separate TV movies by Robert De Niro and Richard Dreyfuss. So here's an idea: If you're going to turn the managing of local government over to private business, think Hollywood. It'll make sure that the bad people get punished, the good people get reelected and meetings will be over in time for "The Late Show with Stephen Colbert."

Vermont pays people to stay — and pay higher taxes

I'm not sure what state officials in Vermont are adding to their famed tree-to-table maple syrup, but they really should cut back on it before the state's workforce shrinks even more.

Vermont has lost 16,000 workers in the past nine years and now has the oldest median age (almost 43 years old) — the third oldest in the nation, according to The Wall Street Journal.

I wouldn't comment on things happening in Vermont if I weren't so fearful that they could happen here. Now, I wouldn't mind if we expanded the state's smallish maple syrup industry — but I don't want California's, much less Sacramento's, economic development tsars to steal Vermont's newest, stupidest idea. Here it is.

If you work remotely for a company not in Vermont — and it really doesn't matter where you do it from — Vermont will give you $10,000 to move your desk and Wi-Fi equipment there. No one need be the wiser where you're texting and Skyping from — except when you file your taxes. And there's the rub. Quoting again from The Wall Street Journal, Vermont's property taxes are the third-highest in the U.S. and "its top marginal income personal rate (is) 8.95 percent."

So, in essence, if you accept the 10,000 smackers to move there, you'll probably find yourself getting smacked into giving it back, possibly in your first year. What amazes me about all of this is that even with my financial-planning skills being roughly comparable to those of a ferret, I'm not tempted to follow up on this offer. Not even "remotely." (For those of you wondering why I choose to compare my fiscal acumen with a ferret's, it's a whimsy based on the fact that when you get a group of these little critters together, they comprise "a business of ferrets." I used that as the title of a novel I wrote a few years ago about Hollywood, by the way, which was rejected with record speed by every publisher and agent who read it. Philistines.)

Don't get me wrong: economic development people can offer all kinds of incentives to lure companies here — from deeply discounting the cost of square footage on office or industrial space to creating affordable rentals and education packages, and cutting red tape on behalf of a company's expansion projects.

What most ED professionals won't do is attempt to seduce companies and individuals to relocate here by promising them they'll be hugely taxed and will lose scores of jobs because workers won't be able to afford the cost of living here.

In summary, I'm not sure why Vermont leaders don't simply lower the state's taxes if they want to staunch an outward flow moving much more rapidly than its justifiably famous maple syrup.

June 19, 2018

What would a Starbucks presidency look like?

Are you as intrigued as I am by the prospect of former Starbucks CEO Howard Schultz running for president of the United States?

So far, Schultz — who also was an owner of the Seattle SuperSonics and is said to be worth at least as much as Donald Trump claims to be — is being a bit reserved about whether he'll toss his apron into the ring. I haven't been this stoked about coy denials of a presidential run since Oprah issued them about her own aspirations. Besides, after the three years of a presidential candidate then actual president who's been the opposite of reserved — "rabid" would come to mind but I like dogs, even if they're foaming at the mouth — it may be that thinking before one speaks, or at least going through the motions of appearing to think before one speaks, would be as refreshing as Starbucks' Nariño 70 Cold Brew with Milk.

As an early voter guide, here are nine things I think we can expect from a Howard Schultz presidency.

1. Access to White House bathrooms — even if you're not there to buy anything, including the candidate's platform.

2. Free Wi-Fi everywhere in the U.S. — even in such remote, web-challenged spots as Death Valley, the Everglades, Egypt and Shingle Springs.

3. A chief executive sufficiently wired to remain awake for early-morning briefings.

4. For voters who thought they wanted a

businessperson in the White House, at last! A true bean counter.

5. The names of everyone on the inauguration invite list will be misspelled.

6. The government will be shut down every few weeks for four-hour teaching moments. (This actually could turn out well. When's the last time anyone on Capitol Hill took the time to learn anything?)

7. The Presidential Medal of Freedom and the Kennedy Center Honors will be replaced by gift cards.

8. Cabinet secretaries and ambassadors will now be called baristas and associates.

9. Not only will the talk of building a wall to separate the U.S. from Mexico be abandoned, but also the president's closest adviser will be Juan Valdez. (Note to younger readers: "Juan Valdez" is a fictitious Colombian coffee farmer created for the National Federation of Coffee Growers of Colombia. For many of us who grew up watching "him" on TV commercials — different actors played him over an almost 60-year period — his dignity first inspired our desire to hold out for good coffee. He was never a cultural stereotype, like the Mexican Frito Bandito, South American Chiquita Banana or debatable life form Jar Jar Binks, who singlehandedly set back the cause of space-alien assimilation at least 50 light years.)

California split isn't even good poker

There's separation of church and state — and then there's separation of state and state (and state!), thanks to a ballot measure by venture capital and bitcoin investor Tim Draper. He hopes voters will agree in November to trisect California into Northern California, Southern California and, I guess what we could call generic California.

We'd be part of the new state of Northern California. Frankly, I think this is just a clever trick to make us solely responsible for the Sacramento Kings. But on the plus side, the measure does throw San Francisco into the mix, which is convenient since half of its people are abandoning it and some of those are moving here.

Also on the plus side, if the measure passes, Fresno would become part of Southern California, which it certainly has never been. But dislocating a place isn't without precedent. In Vacaville's promotional materials many years ago, the city claimed to be part of the Bay Area. This is a way of using geography as a theory. (For comparison's sake, quantum physics is also a theory, but it has a better press agent.)

The third leg of this preposterous stool — and I mean the term to be both metaphorical and scatological — is what I'm calling generic California and what the bitcoin wizard is simply calling California.

With the exception of San Diego and La Jolla, which would be in Southern California, the new-and-improved California would have the state's most expensive beachfront property, from L.A. to Monterey. I wonder how much of that Draper owns. If you think this is starting to sound a little like

107

Lex Luthor's scheme to remove the current state of California from the map in the first "Superman" film with Christopher Reeve — in the process turning Boise, Idaho, into Surf City — you're not far off. Or at least not that farther off than Draper.

This isn't Draper's first mega-rezoning. Only four years ago, he suggested splitting California into six states, which sounded so ridiculous it didn't even qualify for the ballot. There must be a lesson here for would-be politicos. Just as there are rules in comedy — such as "pickle" is a funnier word than "apple," for example — it's evident that breaking up a state into thirds sounds more palatable than breaking it up into sixths (a word I'd love to hear Daffy Duck say). I wonder if Draper put together a focus group on this. I imagine the participants were just bursting with ideas.

"How about turning California into 51 states? Then, all together, the country would have 100. The ad campaign could go, 'Let's get up to 100. Catch the fever!' "

"I hate that. Why not just make Puerto Rico part of California? We could call it Eastern California. Or, in Español, Este California?"

"That's idiotic. Why not call it Este Lauder, while you're at it?"

"It's taken. But as long as we're blue-skying here, I think we should make Israel our 51st state. And Palestine our 52nd. What could possibly go wrong?"

"Thank you all for coming here this morning. I'll take it from here."

"It's your call, Mr. Draper."

"No offense taken, Boss."

Will DST be told to R.I.P.?

C alifornia is thinking of pulling an Arizona by opting out of daylight saving time. Assembly Bill 807 is springing ahead (not falling behind) to make it onto the November ballot.

To clarify: Except for the Navajo Nation, Arizona stays on Mountain Standard Time year-round. People and businesses there collectively decided years ago that it hated, hated, hated DST — probably because it gets so hot in most of the state that the notion of adding another hour of daylight is akin to offering someone crawling out of the desert a tall glass of sand.

DST, as you know, originally was devised to help farmers extend their seasons by lengthening sowing and growing hours. But to those of us who weren't in the ag business, the time change every spring meant nothing more significant than being able to drive home from work and to our kids' soccer, softball and choir practices while it was still light. It also saw us getting up the next morning in pitch black, then driving to work in a sort of lilac dawn — which may sound pretty but not if you're too groggy to drink it in, poetically speaking.

We've had DST in California since the year before I was born so I grew up with it, never having had a sense of what it would be like every spring and summer to not be able to go back outside after dinner to play some more softball. This might have been a mixed blessing, though: We ran out of our homes on full stomachs, since none of us at that age ate "light" or even "healthy" dinners. I recall my father mock-regretting one night that he hadn't bought stock in Pepto Bismol.

But DST also meant we could stay up later, since only cruel parents made their kids head to bed when it was still light outside (unless the kids were still babies or they lived in the Land of the Midnight Sun, in which case there were no alternative options). Since we didn't have school the next day (once summer kicked in), this gave us our first opportunity to watch late-night TV, which had built up in our minds over the years as an exotic pleasure. Which, of course, it rarely was.

Some people consider DST unhealthy — that it messes with our circadian rhythms or, put less mysteriously, our sleep/wake cycles. Or, least mysteriously of all, our internal cuckoo clocks. But, not being a sleep researcher, I have no idea if this stuff is real though doesn't "sleep researcher" sound like a great job? How do they know you're not being productive when you're caught dozing at meetings?

In any event, by the time AB 807 is enacted, if that even happens, we'll probably have gone through another couple of DST periods. In the meantime, I'm preparing my body to deal with it by not going out to play softball after dinner. I'm very adaptive.

HOME AND HARSH

Moving on: The selling of 'Stately Goldmanor'

For the nearly 20 years I owned it, I often called my East Sacramento home "Stately Goldmanor." It was a gag, not a brag: a rather obvious play on my surname. But it was also a wink at the old Batman comic books (and spoofy 1960s TV series), in which any reference to the estate of the caped crusader's alter ego, Bruce Wayne, was always preceded by the adjective "stately."

Located on 40th Street between J and M streets, the house, which I sold this past Thanksgiving Day, is a thoroughly revamped California bungalow that the owner before me—a talented architect named Russ Wall—turned into a 4,800-square-foot mini-mansion. In around 1989, the once humble cottage reemerged as a three-story-plus-full-basement, Art Deco-inspired home. It now had five bedrooms, three-and-a-half baths, a long kitchen reminiscent of a bowling alley lane and exterior decks jutting out from all three floors.

We first saw the place after my wife Jane and I had lost a bid to buy another, more traditional home, also on 40th Street. The seller had moved his family back to Chicago, evidently hated it there—this all occurred in the winter, which I think may be a significant clue—and moved everyone right back to Sacramento.

Disappointed about the deal falling through, Jane and I drove to 40th Street one afternoon to see if there was anything else in the area that we could (barely) afford. We saw a for sale sign farther down the block. Empty for a year-and-a-half, the place looked almost antebellum from the outside, with tall, decorative white pillars and, because

113

of some severe angling, a semi-secreted 10-foot high front door. The home all but begged us to walk up the front steps, press our noses against the windowpane and have a collective, open-mouthed gawk.

What we saw was an open-architecture home with exposed staircases, cruise line-like windows and railings and enough white walls to cause a mild case of snow blindness. "Oh, wow," Jane said, squeezing my arm as her voice trembled a little, "it's a *&$#@* art gallery." (As her friends would attest, Jane tended to the salty at emotional moments. Also in daily speech. It always took people by surprise when this elegantly dressed, lanky woman, a former news anchor with merry sky-blue eyes, swore like a dyspeptic longshoreman.)

Well, it wasn't quite an art gallery yet. But once we bought it and moved in, the art collection we'd been amassing during the first 19 years of our marriage — which we'd crammed into the 1,400-square-foot home near McKinley Park we'd bought from public relations goddess Jean Runyon 13 years earlier — flew onto the walls and floors and sconces in the first two weeks we were there. Spread out on vertical expanses that in some places climbed as high as 35 feet, the paintings finally had breathing room, while the sculptures had enough floor and shelf space to be appreciated rather than stumbled over and skirted around.

For the next 10 years we hosted fundraisers, dinner parties, lectures and even small concerts in our living room, with some attendees, wine glasses in hand, walking up a few stairs and dramatically draping themselves over the banister as though ready for their close-ups in a lifestyle publication. In fact, our home and our art collection became the subject of photo spreads in, among other publications, Sacramento Magazine.

HOME AND HARSH

But the lively canvas of our home and lives had a sad undercoat.

A year after we bought the place, Jane was diagnosed with breast cancer. While we continued to have as much of a social life as her condition would allow us, we spent the next nine years riding a rollercoaster of remissions and returns until she died in January 2007. She was 56 years old; we had lived together for 29 years and four days.

At that time, people asked me if I planned to sell the house, make a fresh start and so forth. One semi-friend accosted me at a deli and solemnly announced, "It takes a year." "What does?" "To properly grieve," she instructed me. I guess I haven't been doing it properly because I'm still grieving, more than a decade, a remarriage and a few relationships later. I told anyone who asked me about moving that no, Jane had loved the place — and the one thing I'd learned from prior tragedies was to not do anything hastily.

Unfortunately, that didn't extend to my remarrying only a year and two weeks later. My new wife wasn't crazy about the house. While raised in a large home herself, she had grown to favor smaller living spaces as an adult. I, on the other hand, had spent the first eight years of my life as one of a family of five in a two-bedroom/one bath apartment in the southeast Bronx section of New York City, where my parents slept on a fold-out sofa in the living room. I loved living in a home I could ramble around in. So we stayed in Stately Goldmanor. The marriage failed and I still stayed, now with just the company of a cat, Osborn the Magnificent, a tubby tabby I'd inherited in the divorce and, as I try to put it chivalrously, an occasional special guest star.

Eventually, things caught up with me. While I continued to make money as a writer, The Great Recession had hobbled my more lucrative consulting business — and for the first time, when I was in the basement and wanted something I'd left on the top floor, I didn't find myself bounding upstairs, two steps at a time, to retrieve it. Instead, I found myself bargaining with me: "How much do you really need those eyeglasses, man? Just squint at the TV." An emotional and physical inertia had begun to set in. After a few failed romances (they all loved the home), I spent more and more evenings at home with Osborn, reading, playing my piano and wondering what, exactly, I'd miss if I sold the place.

The only sweet memories I had recurrently were of dancing in that bowling-alley kitchen with wives and later, lady friends — and of my needing to sleep on the floor in the hall outside my daughter's bedroom for the first two weeks we lived in the house. Jessica had just turned 11 (she's now 31) and was used to her mom and me sleeping in a bedroom just a few feet from hers. Now we were one flight up — and even though it was almost the same distance from her room as before, I'm sure it felt to her that we were light-years away. So, with our Jean Runyon house still on the market at the time, I took Jess there one day so we could measure the difference in footfalls. That seemed to satisfy her, and I was able to return to my own bed that night.

A bittersweet memory I carry with me is of the day that Jessica was married in the backyard, more than five years ago. Jane had always hoped that our daughter's wedding would be at home, and so it was—nearly five years after Jane died. My son-in-law, Joshua Laskey, used his background in theater to arrange the folding chairs into a small outdoor auditorium, including aisles, allowing 150 guests to witness the celebration.

It should have been a joyous occasion but, once again, it had that undercoat of sadness. Not surprisingly, my new wife and I separated a few weeks later.

Once I decided to sell Stately Goldmanor, I went

through two real estate agents — the second one resigned a day after we signed the contract, saying he was "too OCD" to handle my rather unique property—before making the call I should have made at the start: to Polly Sanders, somewhat of a real estate legend in East Sac, whom I had met briefly a few years earlier.

Sanders, 68, is a tall, friendly woman with the same short, distinctive hairstyle and overall "look" that she's had for decades: glamorous but not intimidating. She knows the importance of brand consistency. Her business partner, Elise Brown, who's just 33 years old, dresses for her age: semi-funky, semi-casual but, like Sanders, seriously into snazzy shoes. The added kick is that Sanders has been Brown's stepmother since Brown was four years old; it gives their back-and-forth some generational edge but to my mind, also warmth and mutual respect.

Because I had consulted with a number of real estate developers throughout the years — I had helped market the Serrano Country Club community in El Dorado Hills during its first few years, and more recently came up with the tagline for the downtown Sacramento community The Creamery at Alkali Flat ("Own the City") — I had thought my instincts would guide our campaign to sell my home.

I'm not sure how many ways there are to say that nearly everything I knew was wrong, but I promise to keep trying.

First, Sanders and Brown convinced me to drop my asking price by more than $200,000 since I was selling the home "as-is" (even though I would end up spending a few thousand bucks to address some deferred-maintenance issues). Sanders instructed me to remove everything from the tops of cupboards, tables, counters and credenzas, which I dutifully did. She also told me to "edit" my art collection. "If you have all these sculptures and paintings, people won't be able to see the architecture and envision their own décor,"

117

she said — and, well, I kept meaning to but never did. She told me to be religious about cleaning Osborn's litter box (I obeyed) and refrain from smoking cigars in the basement at night (um, moving right along...).

I think it took fewer than 11 days for a buyer to emerge. The day after the offer was made, countered and accepted, Sanders left for Hawaii for two-and-a-half months—but with her working from there constantly ("just with a better view," she joked), and Brown's turning out to be as busily determined as a border collie, I never felt as though I was underrepresented. Quite the opposite.

A day or two after selling Stately Goldmanor, Brown showed me some town homes in Campus Commons she and Sanders had scouted for me, based on what they now knew about my preferences. I bought the second home Brown showed me one morning. About a third of the size of the home I'd be leaving, it had been owned by two women whose tastes in art and décor nicely mirrored my own. The only challenge is that it has an elegant "island" that runs most of the length of the kitchen. But I think if partners and I shimmy around it just right, we'll still be able to dance there. Here's hoping.

A two-car garage of one's own

I think I've driven in and out of my new two-car garage three times today. And I might be up for a fourth errand shortly. I just love pulling in and out of this garage.

Permit me to explain.

If you live in a home with a garage capable of accommodating a minimum of two cars, you probably have no idea why my now having one has me drenched in giddiness (which is not an especially attractive look for me; fortunately, it rarely presents itself).

Living in East Sacramento since 1978, I'd grown used to the fact that most of the older homes come with one-car garages — and the oldest ones with one-car garages for very skinny cars, circa 1930. Many homes, including the one I lived in from 1983 to 1997, have no garage at all; mine had been converted into a dining room by the previous owner, the late public relations legend Jean Runyon. Fortunately, she dumped the automatic garage-door opener during the remodel; otherwise, my dinner parties would have been windier than usual.

The home I just left on 40th Street, after having lived there a month shy of 20 years, had room for about one-and-a-fifth cars. This is useful if your primary car was made by Toyota and your secondary one by Tonka.

Further, if you're one of those people who like storing garden tools, Christmas lights, wardrobe closets, bicycles, kayaks, golf clubs, Ski-Doos and ossified pets alongside your car, forget it: You'd soon have, as my neighbors and I had, a no-car garage. (In my case, all was not lost. Because my no-car garage had a peaked roof, I had a climate-controlled loft built a few years back, which allowed me to comfortably

119

store paintings, sculptures and rats year-round.)

My new home's two-car garage isn't quite being used as designed.

Until late this morning, it was filled to capacity with boxes — so much so that the movers, apparently taking pity on me, created little aisles for me to slither down, provided I held my breath and didn't intend to tote back with me any treasure I located if larger than a loofah bath mitt.

But today, around 1 p.m., after relentless unpacking (and dumping), the guys managed to shove enough stuff to one side of the garage, allowing me to drive my car into it without fear of door scrapes or no room to exit the vehicle. I must have used the open/close remote 10 times just to ensure that (a) it worked and (b) this wasn't a fever dream.

Well, gotta dash. I need to drive to the grocery store. Or the dentist. Or the movies. Or something.

March 9, 2017

Settling in and getting mail before cocktail time

Readers just like you (though maybe not specifically you) have been emailing me about my recent domestic and business relo from East Sacramento to Campus Commons — or more tellingly, from 4,800 square feet to 1,400 square feet.

I've mentioned it in this space a few times, with my column on having a two-car garage for the first time in decades provoking a slew of emails. I also have an essay about it in the March issue of Sacramento Magazine, which prompted some emails as well as some unexpected bids from real estate agents, who didn't seem to realize I'd sold my home on Thanksgiving Day and bought a new place early in December. Unless I "flip" the latter, I plan to stay put for a while and should be unpacked by 2023.

Anyway, it seems that many of you have moved during the course of your lifetime and related to some of what I wrote about. So I thought I'd jot down a few observations, barely two weeks into my new home/office.

1. The mail is delivered here in the morning. Hallelujah! That's when it's always delivered in TV sitcoms, but on my former block, it would often arrive after cocktails and sometimes dinner (and sometimes, alas, not until the next day). It's the same old mail, of course — but knowing in the morning that I'll have a New Yorker, Economist or Vanity Fair to read that evening puts a little spring in my step the rest of the day.

2. The mail here is slipped through a slot in my detached garage and the newspapers are tossed over the backyard gate. That has a vague rural charm — as do the 11 turkeys that gather at my front door most afternoons. My daughter, the writer Jessica Laskey, says I should view them as a welcome wagon. Hmm. To me, they seem more like a mob of critics waiting to get liquored up and run me out of town. My tubby tabby, Osborn the Magnificent, enjoys sitting on the arm of my chair in the front room and staring them down through the window. I think he thinks they're looking at him, whereas they're simply looking at their own reflection in the glass. These are turkeys, after all, not a delegation from the poultry branch of Mensa.

3. I'm completely unaccustomed to the security touches the ladies who owned the place before me installed, such as lights that suddenly come on when I walk to the garage at night and little chingy-dingy sounds every time I open or close an exterior door, which I guess are meant to frighten tin-eared mice. They also did an expensive, extensive and impeccable remodel that won me over the first time I stepped into the place. You see, I'm not one of those people who buy homes that are in disrepair and enthuse about the possibilities. ("That wall's not weight-bearing. It can go. And then there's that entire back room.") I'm the type who wants to move in and do nothing but unpack for the next few years. Yes, I'm a turnkey turkey.

A saga on the joys of AT&T

I f you move your business or residence, AT&T has some marvelous marketing strategies to get you to give up your landlines with the company.

First, you spend 15 minutes or more on hold, talking to Manly Robo-Voice, who keeps insisting you can use full sentences to explain the purpose of your call. Eventually, since Manly Robo-Voice isn't getting anything you're saying, you start moaning incoherently. That finally gets "him" to say, "Please wait on the line for a customer service representative."

After all, that's all you wanted from the beginning of the call. But you were given no option to ask for a living person.

Just before Living Person does get on the line, a new player, Feminine Robo-Voice, tells you your call "may be monitored for quality assurance." You wish.

So you explain the situation to Living Person: You've moved, you'd like to keep the same number for your business landline but you no longer need separate home and fax lines. You're asked to wait as Living Person does "some checking," forcing you to endure AT&T's sprightly, repetitive on-hold music, which you decide would have been infinitely more effective than waterboarding at the Guantanamo Bay detention camp.

Finally, Living Person comes back on the line and says you can't keep your same business phone number even though you've moved only three miles away and are still in the same city council and board of supervisors districts. But you're feeling a bit cranky so you finally relent and Living Person offers you three choices for a new phone number. You choose the only one you could remember a few moments after Living Person said it, and then the fun starts.

To install a line at your new place, you'll need to make an appointment. "Any time between 8 a.m. and 8 p.m. on Tuesday," Living Person says.

You misunderstand and say, "Oh, well, 10 looks good for me."

"I'm sorry, sir, you don't understand," Living Person says. "I mean the installer will be there sometime between 8 a.m. and 8 p.m."

"You mean," you ask, feeling as though you may have been cast in a remake of Kafka's "The Trial" but no one told you, "that I'm supposed to stay home for 12 hours waiting for the installer?"

"Yes, sir. We never know how long another appointment might —"

"Even Comcast can schedule an appointment in a two-hour window," you say, thinking: And DirectTV probably comes to your house as soon as you hang up the phone. With coffee and doughnuts.

Tomorrow: The saga continues. Please remain on hold. Someone will be right with you.

March 17, 2017

I n yesterday's column, you find out that AT&T grants you a 12-hour "window" if you make an appointment to have a landline installed — specifically, that someone will come do the job "between 8 a.m. and 8 p.m."

So you start lecturing Living Person, the customer rep you waited 15 minutes to reach and finally did so by speaking gibberish to Manly Robo-Voice — the "guy" who said you could speak complete sentences to and who never understood any of them — on all the other phone companies that are out there. You snarkily ask if AT&T has ever used the word "service" in a sentence.

Living Person is getting irritated and possibly rethinking

her career with the phone company. Suddenly she gets an inspiration: "As I look at the records of your new home," she says, "I see there's already a phone jack there. All you have to do is find and plug in your phone, while I activate it from here."

Well, you think, that sounds easy enough. So while Living Person does her thing (which takes another 10 minutes, for some reason), you carry your cellphone with you and look in every nook and cranny of your new home for a phone jack. You never find it, even after Living Person finally signs off and you promise her you'll keep looking. So you contact the former owners of your home, who tell you they took out their landline years ago during the extensive, beautiful remodel they did that ultimately made you want to buy their place.

You dread it but you call AT&T two weeks later — anxiety about doing so has prompted you to delay, in much the way you reschedule dental appointments a few times — and, once you get hold of Another Living Person (after being on hold for 12 minutes), you cancel the whole shebang. "May I ask why?" says Another Living Person, this time a guy who sounds so calm he probably has to put starch in his headset to stay awake for an entire shift.

You tell him the whole saga, making special note of the 12-hour appointment "window." "If I could narrow that to, say, five hours, would you like to keep the new landline?" he asks.

You finally say something completely inappropriate for a newspaper and even a Quentin Tarantino movie. This prompts Another Living Person, who by now knows you're still keeping your AT&T cellphone account, to say he'll waive any charges that accrued during the two weeks you had the nonexistent new landline. "We want to keep you happy," he says. "Tell us what we can do to make you a happy customer."

You tell him what he and his company can do — somewhere between 8 a.m. and 8 p.m.

A hot new idea for VCs: The walk-in litter box

I nvestors, listen up. I have an idea for a product that will see all of us buying yachts, penthouses and our own posses by year's end.

Walk-in litter boxes.

Come on. Hear me out. I realize my previous idea — black dandruff to sprinkle on white summer suits — may have been ahead of its time. But still.

Here's the backgrounder.

My tubby tabby, Osborn the Magnificent, turns 15 on Bastille Day (July 14). Still remarkably agile, he nonetheless has been demonstrating for the past few months a tendency to, um, think outside the box — when he's stressed (in the weeks before we moved to our new home), when he's in an anarchistic mood (in the weeks since we've been in our new home) or, y'know, when he's just being a cat.

If he simply had trouble climbing into the box to "do his thing," as the kids say (especially the ones in their 60s and 70s), I would totally get it. But Osborn manages to run up and down the stairs of our two-story place without any difficulty, just as he did in our previous four-story digs. He's still remarkably fit — more so than his adoptive daddy, for whom opening a recalcitrant jar of olives counts as cardio.

So let's examine the product I have in mind. The only drawback, it seems to me, is how to keep the litter in the box as Osborn tugs open the tiny door to enter. The key would be to have some sort of dam that holds back the litter until Osborn shuts the door behind him — at which time the miniature floodgate would pop open, sending a cascade of clumping sand into the box's "foyer."

Once Osborn has completed his task (I'm almost starting to think this would include reading the newspaper and making political comments), he'd do his usual practice of kicking any sand at his feet behind him. The weight of the litter landing upon the existing litter would trigger a sensor that would slam the teensy floodgate and allow the cat to exit the box.

I believe this is similar to the technology that allows deep-sea divers to enter and exit the below-surface holds of ships and astronauts to get in and out of space shuttles, while orbiting, without bringing back in a small flaming asteroid or alien life form. Kind of an air-lock system. (I'm being way too technical for a prospectus, aren't I?)

I respect you so I'll concede the invention has two primary bugs, to wit:

1. How on earth can anyone train a cat to do anything?

2. See #1 above.

Discovering my cat's been keeping a daily diary

T rade magazines for professional and wannabe writers strenuously recommend against writing articles from your pet's point of view. I think this is sound advice — for everyone else.

In my case, I just discovered that my tubby tabby, Osborn the Magnificent, has been keeping a daily diary for the 10 years he's lived with me. Some secrets are revealed here — but as yet, no evidence of collusion.

By way of background, Osborn turned 15 last Bastille Day but is not, as far as I can determine, remotely French — although he does have a tendency to turn up his nose at most of the movies I watch, unless they're Westerns with chase scenes. He probably buys into the French auteur theory of cinema, that a director is the true author of a film. One of his diary entries makes this point ("Nobody can stampede a cattle drive like John Ford, n'est pa?").

Here are last week's scrawls.

Monday: Woke up at 5 a.m. Meowed loudly at the fat guy who feeds me (FGWFM). He muttered something shocking and turned over. He stirred again at 5:10 a.m., when I repeated the meow. This one was just for fun but he swept me, several pillows and the latest issue of The Economist (which I think helps him get to sleep at night) off the bed with his arm. I then slept most of the day (or was that Tuesday, Wednesday, Thursday, et al.?) on a running shoe he'd left on the floor. Quel slob, non?

Tuesday: Woke up at 5 a.m. Meowed loudly at the FGWFM as though a burglar was in his office downstairs making off with the manuscript for his new musical, "KATZ." It's based on his complete antipathy for the Andrew Lloyd Webber musical whose name sounds the same — but Webber's doesn't feature a Jewish butcher (who feeds the felines in his neighborhood) in the title role. He awoke pretty upset and went downstairs to make coffee. This left his extra-long king bed all to me. Slept 'til noon, got up, stretched, then took it easy for the rest of the day.

Wednesday: Watched though the sliding glass door in the back of the house and chirped along with the birds who were lining up along the rim of a fountain to take little sips of water. FGWFM thought it was really cute until he left the room, and I nosed open the glass door to join the little chirpers. What can I say? It's my nature. I forgot myself. In any event, FGWFM didn't seem appreciative when I brought one of the now-mortally wounded chirpers inside. In fact, for a fat guy with a fairly deep voice, he shrieked like a chimpanzee. I may have to advertise for a new, less high-strung roommate.

Thursday: Watched CNN with the FGWFM. He really doesn't like all the yelling among the guests, but I find it kind of funny. A little like when some of my buddies and I sneak out of our gates late at night and sing together in the alley. (Note to musical-comedy aficionados: We never sing "Memories" from "Cats." We like earthier songs like, "How Dry I Am" and "Down by the Old Mill Stream." Sometimes, we just improvise jazz — you know, me and the other cats.)

Friday: Ate the FGWFM's running shoe for breakfast. The animal experts are right: We cats never use where we sleep as a bathroom. That doesn't mean we don't eat what we sleep on. You might want to jot that down before you go all "rescue" on us.

Saturday: Watched "Saturday Night Live" with the FGWFM, who seems to be spending more time at home with me lately. I think he misplaced or drove off another girlfriend. This one turned out to be allergic — not to me, per se, but to the rose petals I chewed up and spat into her purse. I guess me and FGWFM will watch some Westerns tonight.

No imaginary friend: I have an imaginary slob

A s a kid, I never had an imaginary friend. But as an adult, I have an imaginary slob.

This is the guy who, despite my keeping things spick and span at all times, sneaks into my home, office and car while I'm away and unmakes the bed, unloads the dishwasher to re-dirty the plates, throws my clothes on the floor, smokes cigars and flees just before I get home.

He's canny, this imaginary slob.

He knows I'll find and beat him bloody — okay, I'll issue a stern memo — if he ever messes up the place when I'm expecting a guest. On the other hand, he seems to have a sense of when I'm about to receive a surprise visit from someone, especially if it's a woman who, up to that point, believed my claim of being "a bit of a neatnik." (Why she believed this, after seeing me in my pre-rumpled suits and unruly hair, is inexplicable. Perhaps I've been deluding myself.)

Please understand that an imaginary slob is not the same thing as an inner slob. Almost all of us have the latter. Those of you who also have the discipline to not completely yield to its demands have my greatest respect.

I, on the other hand, have an inner tidy guy. This is a little like having an inner child or, if you battle weight, having a slender person living inside you — which is just an expression, of course. The reality would be like starring in "Alien" or its sequels.

My inner tidy guy has vision. He knows how nice my home, office and car could look with just a little more effort. He's supremely thankful each week after his cleaning professional visits, at which time he unfailingly promises to himself (and his cleaning professional) to keep things just the way she's improved them. He likes what he sees.

But in the first hour after his cleaning professional leaves, he manages to spill coffee while pouring it into his cup. Just a drop or two that lands on the floor. Easy to remedy with a quick swipe of a paper towel. But he can't remember where he keeps the paper towels. So he tells himself, no sweat, he'll look a little later.

And when his cleaning professional shows up a week later, she finds the paper towels immediately and wipes up the now crusty coffee drop. This cleaning professional deserves a medal. She thinks she's cleaning for one man, but we are three: me, my inner slob and my inner tidy guy. Those odds would vex anyone. Even an imaginary friend.

You say tomato, I say rebirth

I thought about my dad one recent hot afternoon as I was planting an heirloom-tomato bush in my new backyard. This is the first time in 20 years I don't have a gardener and, frankly, I wish I hadn't had one sooner. Granted, my backyard now is pretty small compared to the one I had with my previous home. But it's perfectly in scale with my newer, smaller digs. I'd feel like an idiot bringing in someone to tend this English-style garden — a little like hiring a jet plane mechanic to fix a skateboard.

When I look back on my years at the place I kiddingly called Stately Goldmanor, I also realize how little my gardener actually did other than, as the vernacular has it, mow and blow. He once tried to charge me extra during the fall because he had to gather up all of those pesky leaves — to which I countered that this would be fine if I could pay him considerably less in the winter, when the grass went into hibernation and it often rained on the day he was supposed to come by. He saw my point, and the matter was dropped.

He also exhibited remarkable timing. He resigned a few days after my home had sold, without knowing it had. I had been on the verge of telling him I'd no longer need his services, minimal as they'd been.

Even when I had a gardener, if I wanted to plant a tree I usually did it myself — because if I bought one on a Saturday and he wasn't due until the following Thursday, I was fearful that the tree wouldn't last until then. I kept equating the unplanted tree with a landlocked goldfish.

Working in the garden reminds me that doing so, even if it's just a hobby, is an acquired skill, not unlike walking on stilts, in that age may affect your agility but if you ever had

133

the knack for either — I did, for both — and your knees don't quit on you, you can always return to it.

I thought about my dad because for the first 42 years of his life, he lived in apartments in New York City — and not the upscale kind that have charming balconies where you can grow your own zucchini and dill perhaps two months of the year. But in 1958, when he retired from the city's fire department and moved our family to California, we rented a home for a year, then bought our first one. I think only a few days after that, my dad planted a lemon tree in the backyard, which, if bucket lists had existed back then, would have been high on his.

At my last house, I planted a lemon tree that's still yielding after 20 years. At the same time, I planted an orange tree, which produced fat, juicy fruit for 19 years, then cracked and collapsed in a terrible windstorm. I was sad about that — I recalled how many vats of orange juice I'd made in the kitchen when my wife was ill and craved it. My longtime housekeeper noticed it was gone and, with her husband, snuck into my backyard one morning and planted a fig tree in its stead. Shortly thereafter, perhaps coincidentally, I sold the house.

I'm thinking if these tomatoes start to make it, I'm going to head to Talini's Nursery and buy some vegetables and maybe even a lemon or orange tree. Or both. It's nice to start over.

I may even buy some stilts.

A new community with soaring airplanes

The expression "Soaring Ceilings" is commonplace in real estate ads for new homes. "Soaring Airplanes" isn't.

Nonetheless, Greenbriar, a 600-acre, mostly residential community next door to Sacramento International Airport, may start construction as early as next year. According to a recent story by Tony Bizjak in the Sacramento Bee, the builder — Integral Communities of Newport Beach — "plans to build more than 2,400 for-sale houses and nearly 500 rental units, including 200 for lower-income seniors."

Because the project will be built on land used by migrating birds and will contain manmade lakes — maybe they'll call those "artisan lakes" in the ads — it's likely our feathered friends will patronize those water features. That can prove deadly for the birds and hazardous for the airplanes if the former fly or get sucked into the engines of the latter. To be sure, the owners are planning to create steep embankments on the lakes so that the birds have trouble walking in and out of the water — a tactic that somewhat ignores the fact that most birds fly into and out of water. You rarely see them towel off on the shore.

According to the story, "Greenbriar managers ... will be authorized to chase birds off the site using fireworks, scarecrows, water spray and dogs, so that those birds do not set up house around the lakes."

So let's see what we have here.

- A community whose residents will hear airplanes

taking off and landing at all times of the day or night, within a few hundred yards of their homes.

- Impromptu, and, one surmises, startling firecrackers popping off, possibly during the occasional lulls of silence at the airport.

- While scarecrows make no noise, the sound of barking dogs pursuing the birds while those hapless managers spray water at the birds may make the entire environment sound like a scene from a Frankenstein movie, when the villagers rise up and advance on the baron's castle, there to kill the monster he's created. Accordingly, I'd suggest the owners provide the managers with torches.

Since I've helped market communities as varied as Serrano, in El Dorado Hills, and The Creamery at Alkali Flat, I have a couple of ideas for the Greenbriar gang.

1. Market the community to hearing-challenged people.

2. Hire puffins to hide in the bullrushes, then spring out and silently trip birds trying to make their way up those embankments.

3. At a public meeting, invite members of the Sacramento City Council who were in favor of the development to move there, rent-free.

The resulting silence may be deafening.

July 27, 2017

Vacating a storage unit
is a rite of passage

I went through an essential rite of passage last week, one nearly as significant as my bar mitzvah, wedding(s) and the birth of my child: I moved my stuff out of storage and into my garage.

Detritus has left the building.

This doesn't mean I'm done unpacking from my domestic downsizing a few months ago (4,800 to 1,400 square feet). All I really did was just transplant some paintings and bicycles from my near-palatial, climate-controlled unit at Life Storage (on Folsom Boulevard just west of Howe Avenue) to half of my two-car, nonventilated garage about 1 ½ miles away.

I mean it when I say "near-palatial." Some of the storage places I looked at before settling on this one looked like mini Quonset huts, where the breaching of security wouldn't exactly require the services of a master lock-pick. A dog with opposable thumbs and a letter opener could do it.

When I first moved my stuff into Life Storage, one manager told me that the company's video cameras have taped the occasional customer — usually, a guy who'd just been tossed out of his home and marriage — actually sneak-moving himself into his unit in the wee hours. I'm guessing the jig was up when he installed a satellite dish and had a pizza delivered to his unit one night.

Life Storage isn't inexpensive. My extra-large unit — which, as it turns out, was more space than I needed (as was the aforementioned 4,800-square-foot home) — ran $324 a month. That's still cheaper than my monthly homeowners

137

association dues but, to be fair, the unit didn't have a bathroom or access to a swimming pool.

When I was starting to clean things out the other day, I discovered that putting stuff in storage can be addictive. A very nice fellow who rents the unit that was just down the hall from mine was unloading a cartful of boxes. We chatted idly for a moment or two, as middle-aged guys will do once they're convinced the other guy isn't armed or a whole-life insurance salesman. "Moving in or out?" he asked. When I told him I was getting ready to vacate the premises, he actually got a look on his face I'd call wistful. "Yeah, wish I was ready to do that," he said. I asked how long he'd been storing things here. "Eleven years," he said. "It's costly but what're ya gonna do? My wife and I keep buying stuff."

I wondered if that included a satellite dish.

LOCAL FOCALS

Oct. 5, 2016

Pam Marrone's rollercoaster ride is smoothing out

To call the past year a rollercoaster ride for Pam Marrone would be like calling a cyclone a zephyr. Marrone turns 60 on Oct. 14, three days after her biotech company turns 10. The firm, Marrone Bio Innovations Inc., began life at a sprint, its revenues more than doubling year over year. Then, early this year, the Connecticut native found herself testifying before the Securities and Exchange Commission "for three agonizing days" about irregularities in the company's revenue reporting — discoveries that led to the arrest of her former chief operating officer, Hector Absi, on charges of securities fraud. That case is ongoing. Marrone's been absolved of any wrongdoing by the SEC.

Marrone Bio creates pesticides and other agricultural products that rely on environmentally friendly ingredients — "biologicals" — rather than chemicals. The firm went public a little over three years ago, which Marrone says wryly "was a real highlight of my career — until it wasn't." Its initial public offering raised $57 million. Today, she says, because of the SEC troubles, "We're way undervalued."

On the day of this luncheon interview, the company's stock price is $1.83 but has been climbing. The night before our chat, the company won an international Best New Biopesticide award for its Majestene product at the 2016 Agrow Awards held in London. Agrow is an information and research resource for the global crop protection industry.

Marrone (pronounced Mah-ROAN, with a silent "e") says that her principal motivation to get through the past year, was "to make sure that our company's good name was restored."

141

A little later in our chat she reveals why this had strong emotional reverberations for her. "I don't know how many people know this but I named the business for my father," she says. "He was dying (from coronary thrombosis) when I started the company in 2006."

Her father, Ralph Marrone, had been an electrical engineer for Connecticut Light & Power. Pam Marrone recalls how he had built the family home on 40 rural acres as a reflection of his passion for energy efficiency. "The house used passive solar and each room had its own thermostat," Marrone says.

Her mother, Florence, is another example of energy. At 90, she still plants flower bulbs and takes care of the garden at the family home. "I guess I'm a combination of my parents," says the energetic, brisk-talking Marrone, whose business requires frequent globetrotting as she meets with farmers, investors and companies in such non-proximate locales as Ecuador; Saskatchewan, Canada; and Europe; among many others.

Tomorrow: A look at the philosophy that Pam Marrone hopes will literally change the world, one crop at a time.

Oct. 6, 2016

To keep fit, when Pam Marrone is at the Davis home she shares with her husband of 39 years, Michael "Mick" Rogers, Marrone swims for 45 minutes in her solar-heated pool and takes her dogs on two-mile walks and runs during the week.

It's not just to combat the effects of the constant world travel she does on behalf of her company, Marrone Bio Innovations Inc.; it's also because she needs all of her strength to wage war on weeds.

"I won't rest until we solve the problem of weed control," she says over lunch. "It represents the highest cost of organic crop production.

"So here's the vision," she continues. "Most of agricultural products are treated with chemicals, and then some biologicals are dialed in. Why not reverse that? It would be safer and ultimately more cost-effective."

Marrone is one of five children — all of whom remain close, none other of whom work in her field. Her husband, like Marrone, is a cheerful overachiever. He's working on his Ph.D at Smith College's School of Social Work; he already has a master's degree in the field from the University of North Carolina, as well as an MBA from the UC Davis Graduate School of Management.

Among Marrone's current pursuits (besides the war on weeds) is one that should bring a smile to coffee drinkers the world over: finding a way to eradicate the coffee berry borer, an African beetle that can ruin both the yield and taste of the drink.

I ask Marrone how she thinks the pending $66 billion merger of ag industry titans Bayer AG and Monsanto Co. will affect her own company's fortunes. "Funny you should ask," she says. "I was in Paris when the deal was announced. I was looking at the Eiffel Tower, on my way to visit the Louvre and then an incredible dinner when my phone started going off like crazy. I'll tell you what I told everyone who asked: I think it's positive for us. As (the combined) company gets bigger, it also gets slower. Our company is agile. We can get things to market faster."

But will farmers prefer dealing with the seeming security of a monolithic firm rather than one whose current employee count hovers at around 90? "Farmers like to mix and match," she says. "They're smart. They like having choices. I value their opinions, which is why I spend so much time traveling to see how our products are working for them and (listen to) their suggestions. It's actually my favorite part of the business."

Lending an ear to Dean
Sioukas of Magilla Loans

There were two reasons that Dean Sioukas and Chris Meyer christened their free, anonymous search engine — for business owners wanting to borrow money — Magilla Loans.

First, the "whole magilla" is a semi-Yiddish expression that means roughly the same as "the works" (often transliterated as "megillah"). Second, and much more fun, Sioukas says he loves the old Hanna-Barbera cartoon series "Magilla Gorilla," which first aired in the early to mid-1960s. (Since he'll be only 46 in March, he must have caught the show in reruns.)

A distinction that needs to be made immediately is that Magilla Loans is not an online lender. It's a service to which loan officers at banks around the country subscribe, giving mutual access to borrower and lender. At present, those institutions include Wells Fargo, Bank of America, Bank of the West, Umpqua Bank, Golden Pacific Bank and Rabobank, among others, Sioukas says. He also says that since Magilla's launch in September of 2015, $1.4 billion in transactions has come through the system. "I'm kind of amazed," he says, his eyes wide and his mouth slightly agape.

Sioukas, a real estate attorney, and Meyer, who owns funeral homes and has been a Hollywood writer, formed Magilla when the latter wanted to buy a mortuary but was daunted by the amount of time he'd have to spend finding a lender. "I told Chris, 'Dude, just use a search engine,' " Sioukas recalls. "Then I felt really stupid. I tried to find one that wouldn't require Chris to enter all of his private data online, and it didn't exist."

The day before this lunch interview, I went to Magilla's website, which Sioukas built "and even coded" — again, his face registers childlike amazement that he was able to do such a thing without any earlier affinity for information technology. (Now, he says, he's everybody's go-to tech guy.) I pretended I was looking for a business loan. I liked the ease of the prompts, the nonjargon friendliness of the language and, best of all, the anonymity. The idea was that if I wanted to borrow a certain amount of money for a specific project, and I'd provide basic pro forma data, one of the subscribing loan officers might review my information and then get back to me. At that point, if the transaction were to begin in earnest, anonymity would be dropped, of course — though Sioukas and Meyer still wouldn't have the names and numbers.

Sioukas likens Magilla to dating services "except that instead of a mate you're looking for money."

Already successful in their respective fields — Sioukas' family owned the 40 acres on which Amazon.com is building its new fulfillment center in North Natomas — the two now work "pretty much full-time" growing Magilla, which has nine employees in an office near Pavilions shopping center.

Sioukas is a vocal sound-alike for Peter Sagal, the witty host of National Public Radio's "Wait, Wait, Don't Tell Me." He's disarming about his story being no Horatio Alger up-from-the-bootstraps saga. "I'd love to tell you that Chris and I came up with this when we were 18 years old and working in our parents' garage but that's just not the case. My family and my wife's family (the Pappases) worked very hard and became very successful in real estate development here. In Greek families, everyone's involved and everyone's been generous in helping us get this off the ground."

I guess they're into the whole magilla.

Patti Brown helps cancer patients conquer fear

Spend just an hour with Patti Brown, the founder and executive director of Wellness Within Cancer Support Services, and you can see why most of the roughly 250 clients she works with from throughout the Sacramento region each month trust her immediately with their inner lives.

Brown's clients, whom she sees at a tidy house just off Roseville's historic main drag, Vernon Street, are current and former cancer patients trying to live with the fear and anxiety that can ravage their self confidence and courage as surely as the disease can affect their bodies. Soft-spoken with warm hazel eyes that seem at once empathetic and cheerful, Brown converted the office of her marriage and family therapy practice into Wellness Within's inviting space six-and-a-half years ago.

"There's a big difference you feel between driving here and driving to a hospital," she said one recent morning. "Hospitals are wonderful for medical treatment but people (who are) already frightened may get even more nervous going to a formal institution." In fact, major Sacramento area hospitals refer patients to Wellness Within.

Once there, a variety of classes, talks and therapies, such as yoga and meditation, are available, as is a lending library of self-help and -actualization books. And here's the part that often surprises and thrills Wellness Within's clients: Everything is absolutely free.

Wellness Within — which considers its clients to not only be cancer patients and survivors but also their families

— relies entirely on grants and donations to sustain itself. It holds an annual gala in the fall at the Rocklin Event Center, and a farm-to-table event in June.

"We encourage people to be the authors of their own lives, since cancer frequently takes away that ability," Brown said. "We help them learn that they're not the sum total of their disease at a time when everything seems like a blur to them."

Sharon Camissa, who helped arrange this interview with Brown, seconds that notion. "I felt as though I was a hostage to my fear when I was diagnosed with stage 3 melanoma" in November 2013, she said. At the time, she was employed by Sacramento Superior Court to help judges manage criminal cases with defendants who represented themselves. Prior to that, she had spent 20 years as a public defender. "My whole body felt tense — not because of the cancer but because I was so afraid," she added.

A close friend knew about and took her to Wellness Within, a visit that ultimately turned transformative. "I needed some convincing," she said with a smile.

"It's the 'woo-woo' element," Brown said, and both women laughed. "We're just starting to fully appreciate the mind-body connection in our culture."

The Journal of Clinical Psychology backs that up in a recent article: "Along with the vital signs of temperature, respiration, heart rate, blood pressure and pain, it is time for health care professionals to recognize emotional distress as a core indicator of a patient's health and well-being."

Sounds like a good thing to keep in mind. And body.

Sutter CEO Dave Cheney has big plans for the downtown hospital

D ave Cheney, the still-new CEO of Sutter Medical Center, told attendees at a private luncheon yesterday that it does "absolutely no good to predict what's going to happen" with the American Health Care Act, a topic on everyone's mind today as Congress begins to grapple with its passage.

"In previous administrations, you had a pretty good idea of how things were going to go by the time of the inauguration," he tells members of the Sutter Medical Foundation, "or at least a few months down the line." With this administration, he says, making it clear that he isn't saying anything political, "we're pretty much down to (things changing on) an hourly basis."

We do know, he adds, that "things will change and have changed in Washington. The government is not going to be giving us more money. That seems certain. All we can do is keep our focus."

Cheney strikes me as an affable administrator, even when he knows a semi-journalist is in the room — the only person writing down what he's saying. I've been sure to let him know I'm doing just that and his response is a grin that seems to say, Why are we even discussing this?

Everyone I've spoken to about him applauds Cheney's openness and accessibility. Since being hired in January, he estimates he's met with 650 Sutter employees, with some meet-and-greets starting as early as 4:30 a.m. to accommodate the 24/7 operating hours of a hospital.

He's also been getting out in the community, speaking

to a diversity of groups, businesspeople and individuals about Sutter, and doing that rare and wondrous thing that serious leaders do: listening. He says the only way for Sutter to become one of the top five hospitals in the country — it's been listed in the top 100 five times in the past 15 years by Truven Health Analytics — is for it to "have a tight connection to the community." That's why he says "I almost cried" when Sutter committed up to $5 million a year for the next three years to help the homeless, joining Mayor Darrell Steinberg's ongoing initiative to alleviate and maybe even solve the problem. (Sutter also has said it would help fundraise an additional $5 million from the private sector to provide homeless services in Sacramento.)

"This is the uniqueness of Sutter," Cheney says. "There's a real passion here (accompanied by) an incredibly talented medical staff." Passion, he says, is the additional ingredient that makes you a top-five hospital, "which I hope to see us get to in the next few years."

Among the innovations being planned by Sutter are a food-allergy clinic and the creation of a clothes closet for impoverished patients when they're discharged from the hospital.

On the lighter side, Cheney is asked if he has a favorite local restaurant yet. "Every Thursday night I go to — and I hope I'm pronouncing this right — Mikuni" he says, then adds, "You've got to try the rainbow roll. Man!"

Meet the woman putting gurrrl in Girl Scout

L inda Farley tells me during lunch that one out of every two women I meet was probably a Girl Scout at one time. I tell her that sounds like there's a world domination plan afoot and she smiles enigmatically — as if to say: maybe there could be. Gurrrl Scouts, anyone?

Farley has been the CEO of Girl Scouts Heart of Central California for more than four years. She has the upbeat outlook and friendliness you'd expect from someone who's been involved with scouting since childhood (not to mention her stint at Up with People, but more on that in a moment).

It's an attitude and way of life I find all the more remarkable because the day we meet, she's just endured a horrific year — during which her father, mother and one of her two sisters died, the latter just weeks before our interview.

Perhaps one of her personal mantras has helped her handle the recent sadness. "I've always been attracted to change," she says. She's talking about management but it's clear that agility — moving on — may be her greatest coping mechanism.

If Farley's name and face are familiar to you, it could be from her years as development director for the Crocker Art Museum. She also was the chief fund development officer for a chapter of the American Red Cross and "also spent time," as her résumé puts it, as chief operating officer for Up with People, the endlessly perky youth chorale that toured the nation and the world in the 1970s and 1980s — a deliberate counterpoint to the country's anti-Vietnam War era of student protests.

Two things occur a few days after this interview that may be worth mentioning.

The first is that I visit Farley at her Sacramento headquarters on Elvas Way and am taken aback by its size, the scope of the programs offered there and Farley's plans to tear down buildings on adjacent property — which her organization owns, along with the headquarters itself — and build an outdoor "wilderness" retreat in the next couple of years.

The second is that by then I've tested her comment that one out of every two women I meet has probably been a Girl Scout at one time. I ask eight women over the course of a few days. Five, not four, were Girl Scouts. I repeat, a world domination plan is afoot.

In tomorrow's column, we'll see where all these changes STEM from. Please grab a thin-mint cookie and join us.

Sept. 13, 2017

Eighteen counties are affiliated with Girl Scouts Heart of Central California, at which Linda Farley, whom we met in yesterday's column, serves as CEO.

"We cover from Yuba City to the north, Los Banos to the south, Davis to the west and on east into the foothills, where we're very active but have fewer members there," she says. "In rural areas, we're kind of spread out."

Farley says her Girl Scouts council territory draws about 18,000 girls from kindergarten through 12th grade. She also oversees 85 employees and 7,000 "active" volunteers. She smiles and adds, "Please remember I said 'active.' " There are eight councils in California and 112 in the country.

To rephrase a cliché, this isn't your mom's or grandma's Girl Scouts. While the organization always has prided itself on teaching girls to be self-reliant and good citizens, there's

been an increasing emphasis on offering STEM programs
— the hottest new acronym for curricula devoted to science,
technology, engineering and math. Courses are taught at
the Girl Scouts' Elvas Avenue headquarters, a cavernous
administration and activities space owned by Farley's group.
Back when the council was known as Girl Scouts of Tierra Del
Oro, it also had a knack for acquiring real estate. The council
now owns 400 acres just outside Placerville and another 100
in Calaveras County — and, as mentioned yesterday also is
about to raze some buildings adjacent to its Elvas HQ and
develop an interactive "wilderness experience" for the girls.
She says the group also is creating "maker space" labs at
Elvas "for learning about robotics, computer coding and other
technology."

"Did you know that every female U.S. secretary of state
is a former Girl Scout?" Farley asks me during our initial
sit-down. "Did you know we have something like six million
alumnae?" For a group that's been this pervasive for 105 years,
that's not terribly surprising. And since Girl Scouts continues
to reinvent itself, it's also encouraging that 100-some years
from now the alumnae ranks will swell.

One thing remains the same, however. In addition to
grants and donations, the biggest revenue producer for
Girl Scouts remains the sale of Girl Scouts cookies. At our
interview, Farley has brought along a box of thin mints and its
newish concoction, S'mores, which are essentially chocolate
and marshmallow graham cookies. I'm about to decline the
gift when I realize I can regift them. So I give the thin mints
to my cleaning lady, who says they're her faves. I put the
other box in my refrigerator and decide to sample one while
watching a movie the other night. Suddenly, five of them have
disappeared. By week's end, they've all vanished.

"Well, that's certainly a mystery," Farley says with a smirk
when I tell her. "S'more or less," I think but don't say.

Rev. James Trapp's vision
of virtual congregations

R ev. James Trapp is a respected, even beloved man of
God. He also believes fervently, though certainly not
to the same extent, in the power of marketing.

"That's what we need to do, plain and simple, at SLC,
market our message and mission to people we don't usually
reach," he says over lunch recently.

SLC is Spiritual Life Center, a nondenominational house
of worship at 2201 Park Towne Circle. Founded almost 20
years ago, it draws between 200 and 250 people every week,
he says, "a number I'd like to see reach 1,000."

His official title, since joining the church five years ago,
is senior minister of worship.

He previously spent seven years as president and CEO of
Unity Worldwide Ministries, based in Kansas City, Missouri.
For nine years prior to that, he was the senior minister of
South Florida's Unity on the Bay, a congregation he says he
helped grow from 100 to 1,200 attendees per week.

In Sacramento, Trapp is the African-American leader
of a mostly white, middle-aged-and-older congregation. The
lack of diversity as well as unavoidable attrition will threaten
the center's survival at some point, he acknowledges.

It's why, with a church committee, he's been reaching
out via social media to a potential membership of younger
worshipers from various cultures.

"Millennials and other young working professionals
don't necessarily need to go into a building on a strict
schedule to have a relationship with God," he says. "They
might want to communicate with their minister and fellow

congregants online, and at various hours."

He leans in slightly to make his point. But that hypnotic voice of his — rich, melodic and warm rather than summoning hellfire and brimstone— hardly requires his leaning in. (If this were the movie "Jerry McGuire," my line would be "You had me at millennials.")

"The church is changing and we have to respect that," he says. "My generation grew up in the church and that was an actual building. Today, some of the mega-churches are doing well but attendance in small- and mid-sized churches like ours are plateauing. We need to find another way."

Tomorrow, Trapp springs that other way. Please file in.

Sept. 19, 2017

"P eople still want and need God," Rev. James Trapp of Sacramento's Spiritual Life Center says. "They just don't want or need the walls. We have to start virtual congregations."

It's a doable transition, Trapp says, since his flock "doesn't see the Bible as a literal document. We see it as allegorical. We read the stories and parables and apply a metaphysical interpretation. So why can't we see the church as something that doesn't always need to be literal brick and mortar? For those who need that, we'll always have it. For those who find a different way to God — young people, people of all cultures, who may not need the traditional structure — we want to be there for them as well."

The eldest of his seven siblings, Trapp majored in economics at Princeton University, from which he graduated in 1974. For a time he worked in the business department of the Miami Herald newspaper. After earning his law degree at the University of Florida, he was working as a criminal defense attorney "until my life went off the rails," he says.

154

"Lots of drugs and alcohol. These were the cocaine cowboy days in Miami, and I found myself caught up in it."

Then, he says, a friend he met in rehab suggested Trapp attend a service at Unity on the Bay, also in Florida. "I told him, 'You don't get it: I don't do church. I'll go this one time if you don't bother me about it anymore.' I sat by the back door in case I wanted to leave in a hurry."

But something happened that day, he recalls. "In my mind, the minister wasn't just giving a sermon. In my mind, he wasn't even talking to the rest of the congregation," he says. "It was like he was talking to me. Just to me. Like he knew me and knew what I needed." Trapp smiles and slightly raises his voice. "I should have sued him for invasion of privacy!"

He began helping out at the church and before long rose to the ranks of assistant minister, then senior minister.

Trapp, who's 65, has been married for 20 years. His wife, Angela, works for Sutter Health as a leadership consultant. Their son, Jaelan Mandela Trapp, is a student at Howard University.

Trapp is writing a book with the intriguing title, "There is No God Like That" and he still seems surprised by where life has taken him. "If someone had told me a few years earlier that there were a thousand things I might do with my life, this wouldn't have been one of them," he says. "But here I am — and it's definitely who I am."

Burnett Miller Park is dedicated (and deservedly)

They named a beautiful little patch of AstroTurf, sod, playground equipment and local art in East Sacramento in honor of Burnett Miller Saturday, in the year-old McKinley Village.

It was notable for how much affection and humor punctuated the remarks of people who've known, worked and laughed with Burney, as everyone calls him, for decades — as well as the all-star cast of elected and appointed leaders who showed up to pay tribute to the former mayor, city councilman, World War II hero (featured in Ken Burns's documentary, "The War"), and businessman (his family lumber company, Burnett & Sons, is close to 150 years old). The speakers included:

- The village's developer, former state Treasurer Phil Angelides, who mentioned at least twice that he'd lost the election to represent the city's District 3 to Miller years ago (and said he's finally out of politics "by popular demand" — a funny line, but don't count on it).

- Legendary artist Wayne Thiebaud, the nonagenarian who still plays tennis with the nonagenarian Miller several times a week at Sutter Lawn Tennis Club, which ought to cause a run on racquets and white shorts at REI. Thiebaud lauded Burnie and wife Mimi's longtime support of the arts, including their great collection of the works of Northern California artists. Then he mock-praised his very close friends for showing "the exquisite taste to not collect me.

- Burnett himself who, after listening to the praise — from the aforementioned, as well as Councilman Jeff Harris, U.S. Rep. Doris Matsui, Mayor Darrell Steinberg and Angelides — said, in his best sardonic voice, "After hearing all this I thought, well, maybe I really am wonderful. I didn't feel that way when I came here today, but I might as well cave in."

It was nice that all of them recognized the event was to honor Miller, in contrast to Larry Webb's comments, which were funny but mainly about Larry Webb and the community. Webb's firm, The New Home Co., was Angelides's partner in the 10-year struggle to create McKinley Village. We learned from his comments that he'd just flown up here from Orange County that morning and had never met the man of the hour until right before the ceremony but "was told" he "kicked ass." Or something. He also lavished praise on Angelo Tsakopoulos, a most admirable man who was in the audience but, uh, wasn't the honoree.

I need to mention that until February, I was privileged to live across the street from Burnett and Mimi Miller. In fact, I've known them 41 years this week, since he was on the Sacramento City Council when I was hired by now-retired city manager Walter Slipe (who was also at the event — along with Judge Ron Robie and his wife, Lynn, the former city councilwoman; former Mayor Heather Fargo; Judge Kim Mueller; former city manager Bill Edgar; artist Fred Dalkey and his wife Victoria, the longtime Sacramento Bee arts critic. The list could go on.

So could my emotions. I often appreciate the kick-start my own career got in 1976 by being brought up here to work with some truly extraordinary people. I was thrilled to see them all still standing.

The snark in me needs to mention that for all of

Ed Goldman: Don't Cry For Me, Ardent Reader

McKinley Village's splendors, Angelides, who recently bought one of his own homes here, really ought to consider investing in a working microphone. The one used at the ceremony went dead every fourth word or so (only Matsui seemed to know exactly how to hold and use it; at least 85 percent of what she said was audible). For a community with such potential, I think it'd be (here it comes) a pretty sound investment.

(Author's Note: Burnett Miller passed away peacefully on Oct. 14, 2018 at the age of 95, in his living room, surrounded by his family. I wrote about this extraordinary man — a friend for 42 years and my across-the-street neighbor for 20 years — in a column that ran online Oct.16 in the Sacramento Business Journal and, in a condensed version, in print on Oct. 19.)

Oct. 23, 2017

Meet low-profile/high-octane Michael Tate

At one of the more successful Sacramento-based wealth management firms you may never have heard of, something's been changing but really not that much. Is there a story here and, more to the point, have I succeeded in aggravating you?

I'm sorry. It's just that The Tate Group, a newly branded entity that combines two previous, well-established and highly regarded companies under the same founders and managers, has never marketed itself. At all. Its website has been negligible, and bios and photos of the principals are apparently an afterthought.

"We never really needed to ask for business," says Michael Tate. "It's all been by referral."

These must have been pretty serious referrals. The 15-member company does business up and down California but also has "a handful of clients in New York" — and, Tate says, "a lot of clients in Washington, D.C." Smiling, he says, "We started with just one. I guess we did a good job and he told his friends."

At 44, Tate recently was named the managing principal of the firm founded by his still-very-active dad, Robert Tate. It wasn't really a coronation. Tate the younger has been steering the firm's management teams for quite some time — quietly.

I have to take you aside for a moment and tell you that Michael Tate — along with his wife Jessica and his young sons, Alexander and Parker — lived next door to me in East Sacramento for several years. He moved away before I did, and the family is now ensconced in a home in Arden Park.

But that's not how I came to be sitting with him over lunch on this balmy, autumn afternoon at the Sutter Club. We'd been brought together by a third party who had no idea we'd been neighbors.

Except for the fiduciary nature of his work, Tate isn't someone you'd immediately say was born to be low-key. Tall and athletic, with a richly deep voice, he looks like the kind of guy who should be playing a wealth management adviser in TV spots or even a daily soap opera ("As The Derivatives Turn" comes to mind). He laughs easily, smiles regularly and for a guy who awakens every morning at 4:30 and is in the office an hour later to deal with the time difference for his East Coast clientele, he seems remarkably cheerful. After recapping his daily schedule, which includes being in bed not all that early each night, he jokes, "Yeah, I'm tired. Really tired."

He has a funny way of showing it. When the Tate firm had a client with "a little too much cash on hand," Tate and his team suggested the decidedly urban client delve into investing in agriculture. "I didn't know anything about the ins and outs of farming, but as a business, it seemed like it would pencil out," Tate recalls. So he did his research, finding that rice farming was a "usually immediate way" to start making money from the start, since planting and growing fruit trees would take a longer time to yield profits.

Then, not content to have simply read about farming, Tate hit the road, driving to rice farms throughout the region and talking to growers about the realities of their business. "There's just no substitute for learning these things face-to-face from the people who've devoted their lives to it," he says.

I ask Tate how it is working side by side with his dad. "Well, it's great," he says, "but if we ever disagree about something, we call in management to mediate." Management?

Sheila Boxley chalks up 20 years with the CAP Center

Unlike many social service organizations, Sheila Boxley says the Child Abuse Prevention Center calls the people it helps "families we work with. We don't call them clients, patients or victims."

Boxley is about to celebrate her 20th year as president and CEO of the CAP Center, just as the statewide, nongovernmental agency is poised to commemorate its own 40th anniversary in 2018. To that end, the center is currently on a quest to find sponsors for a major fundraising event it will hold in late April, which happens to be Child Abuse Prevention Month. Boxley says that while the event will "definitely be for adults," it will be both casual and feature kid-friendly activities. She laughs when I ask if this will include a bounce house — but now that I think of it, she neither denies nor confirms it.

The CAP Center, which began with a staff of three and "a tendency to treat child abuse after the fact," Boxley says, now has 50 employees and 350 partnering agencies, including community service organizations such as AmeriCorps and VISTA (with a combined volunteer membership in California alone of more than 400).

The CAP Center's physical plant is used strictly for administration and training, Boxley says. It's located in North Highlands, just down the block from the entry to McClellan Business Park, the former U.S. Air Force base that was decommissioned and repurposed more than 14 years ago. I mention this because it's gratifying to see how much private- and public-sector activity the conversion has spurred in and around the former military installation.

Boxley is the CEO of all the organizations under the CAP Center's umbrella, and answers to a single 25-member board of directors. "I'm their only employee," she says with a slight smile, "which keeps things a little less complicated."

The CAP Center sends representatives into homes to work with at-risk families — in other words, with those whose socioeconomic or personal circumstances could lead to child abuse. The goal is to head off children from entering into the child welfare system by providing counseling and other forms of assistance.

Boxley, 65, projects warmth, a sense of humor and a lifelong commitment to service — which, in retrospect, seems somewhat inevitable. "My folks were very active people who always served in their community," she says one recent afternoon as we sit in the center's low-key conference room. In fact, she adds, "My whole family was into serving. For 40 years, my aunt ran the annual Red Cross blood drive." Her late father was a city councilman in her hometown of Marked Tree, Arkansas, and her mom, who'll turn 90 early next year, was a schoolteacher for many years.

She and longtime partner John Hodgson, a developer with whom she lives in Sacramento's midtown, are bicyclists, hikers and joggers. (A good thing, too, since Boxley says she's passionate about cooking.)

Boxley has two grown children: Mark, 33, who works in San Francisco's financial industry, and Reid, 27, who works for Sacramento Steps Forward, one of the region's respected homeless-assistance organizations. "He definitely inherited the do-gooder gene," she says.

Dec. 27, 2017

Meet Patty Kleinknecht,
steward of the River District

Since 2005, Patty Kleinknecht has been performing impossible feats of dexterity, tact and grace as executive director of the River District, a conglomeration of properties just north of downtown Sacramento. Its boundaries contain everything from light industrial to Loaves and Fishes, from the headquarters for Yellow Cab Co. to Blue Diamond Almonds, and from the residential development Township Nine to Goldies Adult Superstore (which, contrary to its name, doesn't sell adults). Is this what planners mean when they call an area "mixed-use?"

Kleinknecht's job is to be the steward, herder or referee (pick your metaphor) of all these interests and owners, as well as those of her 15-member board of directors, all the while keeping the district's needs on the radar of the city of Sacramento's elected and appointed officials, public safety and planning departments. And while she's not tasked with soliciting new business tenants for the district, she makes sure that its possibilities are fully appreciated by business development people, such as the Greater Sacramento Economic Council.

The district's expansion hasn't always been fast-tracked. But it isn't intended to be. "Developing this area has always been a marathon, not a sprint," Kleinknecht tells me over lunch recently. "We're not a collection of storefront businesses. Almost everything that comes here has a larger footprint, and that takes time and planning."

She knows all about both of those. From 1992 until she was hired for her current job, Kleinknecht served as general manager of the Dallas Downtown Improvement District, where she created a number of programs to focus attention on businesses there, notably the commissioning of two 12-story murals and a free weekly concert series. Prior to that, she held real estate management positions at three private-sector Dallas companies.

The River District used to be called the Capitol Station District when it was envisioned that it would someday house a multimodal transportation hub. Didn't happen. It's been a PBID since 1999: a property-based improvement district. If a majority of property owners agree, a PBID requires them to tax themselves to fund enhancements and day-to-day maintenance, which includes safety.

Fairly unusual for this particular PBID is that in the River District, many of the property owners also own the businesses that occupy their parcels and buildings. In other PBIDs, scattered across Sacramento County, property owners are principally the landlords for enterprises owned by others.

The River District has become a stew of old and new enterprises, including the California Lottery headquarters, the transplanted-from-downtown Greyhound Bus station and Vintage Monkey, which isn't exactly your father's motorcycle repair shop (unless it happened to have a cafe and retail).

Kleinknecht's mom, Pat, lives in Texas, is 92 and "remains very independent." Her sister Linda and brother Fred are retired from retail and engineering, respectively.

Then there was her dad. Partly because of him, Kleinknecht says she's especially excited about the prospect that the city's new Powerhouse Science Center, a former PG&E plant next to the Sacramento River, may finally start construction after years of stop-go financing challenges. Her father Kenneth Kleinknecht, who died in 2007, worked for NASA in executive positions "for all of the U.S. space projects," she proudly recalls. "I got my sense of detail and my work ethic from him. He'd have been thrilled to see this project come together."

And if that happens, the River District's already charmingly eclectic mixture of businesses finally will be out of this world.

Tim Hemmen is straight ahead on reverse mortgages

Tim Hemmen thinks I've got it all wrong about reverse mortgages. Quite possibly — even though I had one and he hasn't (though he says he "most certainly will" get one when he's old enough to qualify in a few short years). I also should mention that Hemmen sells mortgages for a living.

But he makes a pretty good case for them as "instruments" (as financial people like to call things that emit no music whatsoever), especially for those who don't necessarily need the money but want it to be close at hand once they retire. "A lot of people get to the point in their lives at which they're house-rich but cash-poor," he says at a recent lunch.

Are you still unfamiliar with how a reverse mortgage works? If so, you've managed to avoid the relentless onslaught of infomercials, mailers, email blasts, robocalls, print advertorials and sometimes negative word-of-mouth (to which I plead guilty, but stick with me for a moment; I have the capacity to change, as Michael Corleone once said).

In a nutshell, as you approach the age of 62, or once you've passed it, you can apply for a reverse mortgage — as a line of credit, monthly payments or a lump sum — based on the equity in your home, even if you've paid it off. You can run the money out to pay off debts (as I stupidly did), thereby leaving you with a huge new debt (as I stupidly acquired). You can try to pay it back (as I finally did, before and after selling my former home). Or — and this is a key point — you can just leave it alone and know it's there in case of an emergency.

If you stay in your home for the rest of your life (which I didn't do), and even spend all the dough (which, as we've learned, I did do), after you die the mortgage holder, which usually isn't the entity at which you originated the loan, then swoops in (um... make that comes forward) to reclaim its money from the presumed sale of your home. If you've left the home to your kids or cockatoo, they can stay but they have to pay back the loan. And during the time you have the loan, you're still responsible for paying the property taxes, utilities and so forth — and using the home as your actual residence.

I ask Hemmen if the new tax bill will have a chilling effect on reverse mortgages. "Not significantly," he says, "but it'll be interesting to watch the 'domino effect' of the tax law changes as it impacts real estate.

"If real estate prices drop," he continues, "then the amount of equity that's available will be less. Tax-wise, this may be a little over my head. But I'm watching to see how all the death taxes, like inheritance, estate and capital gains, are finalized and what that means to heirs of the estate." He thinks those heirs "may be able to write off the interest on a reverse mortgage after it's been sold and the loan repaid. "But, he adds, cautiously, "stay tuned."

Hemmen has been in the real estate field for 33 years. After graduating from college and obtaining his real estate license, he worked as a loan officer and a leasing agent for different companies. He got into the reverse mortgage game (notice I didn't say "racket") just last year, working for the American Pacific Reverse Mortgage Group, at its Roseville headquarters. The company is ranked No. 22 in the country for how many loans it's originated.

I should point out that Hemmen was a student of mine once or twice at California State University Sacramento when

I was an adjunct something-or-other in the latter part of the 1980s. And that I like him: He's good company, a caring dad of two grown daughters and a devoted husband of 25 years. He and his wife, Angela Gitt, a top producer at Lyon Real Estate, live in Gold River.

Hemmen makes the reverse mortgage sound like a viable alternative to taking out standard second mortgages. As we talk, I make no bones about the fact that I did everything wrong when I had one. He smiles and says, "The reverse mortgage is just a vehicle. It's the person driving the vehicle who can make it work or not." Mine, of course, was a driverless one. But who knows? If I need some money, I may just go out and kick a few tires again.

Katherine Bardis: A champion equestrian jumps into building

I f things had worked out differently, Katherine Bardis would have been jumping show horses at the Olympics instead of jumping through hoops as a successful homebuilder.

Bardis is the co-founder (with cousin Rachel Bardis) of Bardis Homes, a six-year-old company that already has built more than 200 homes and, according to the company, garnered $100 million in sales. Her signature infill projects — some well underway, some about to happen — include The Mill at Broadway; The Good Project and The Savoy, both in West Sacramento; and Fair Oaks EcoHousing.

At just 30 years old, Bardis defies the stereotype of rudderless millennials. "Everything written about my generation is just plain wrong," she says in a firm, just-try-to-challenge-me voice, offset by a broad smile.

"Millennials represent a generation of tragedy," she continues. "We've experienced 9/11, the huge economic downturn, violence." She pauses to summarize. "I think we're a wary generation but we're definitely not lazy. In my work, I've cleaned toilets and painted walls with my cousin. We're a dynamic duo."

When Bardis was younger, she was "absolutely passionate about horses and thought that riding and jumping would be what I did with my life," she says over lunch at the Sutter Club. She was talented enough riding English style to be on the U.S. pre-Olympics equestrian team for show jumping — but realized she couldn't do that and also go to law school. "I knew I'd need to neglect the jumping if I concentrated on my classes."

Yes, Bardis is also a McGeorge School of Law graduate who clerked for Somach, Simmons & Dunn, a highly regarded firm that specializes in, among other things, land use. But she never practiced. "I really think I went to law school so I'd better understand things as a builder," she says.

That was, after all, the family business. The only child of developer Chris Bardis (who remains professionally active in his early 80s, according to his proud progeny), she worked with her dad at Reynen & Bardis Homes, which has built more than 10,000 homes in California and Nevada.

Bardis majored in communications at Loyola Marymount College in Southern California. Her sense of branding, whether learned or refined in school, is admirable. She pitches homes at The Mill, targeted to young buyers, as "obtainable living" instead of "affordable housing." "Affordable" may be a useful description for public housing but tends toward the toxic for market-rate private homes, evoking the controversial acronym NIMBY (Not In My Backyard). In fact, "A lot of our homes don't even have backyards," Bardis says. "The idea is that people will spend time with their neighbors — an old-fashioned but important thing to do."

Tomorrow, Bardis discusses her building philosophy and looks at that most uncertain project of all: the future. Please begin lining up along the driveway.

March 6, 2018

Being young and female, Katherine Bardis has experienced her share of age and sex discrimination, despite her enviable accomplishments as a builder.

"Ageism compels me to just be better at what I do," she says. "It motivates me to be better, to try harder. I've sat at banks for hours trying to do wire transfers, which really should be pretty simple when you're established as a builder. I had to go through them triple-checking my assets and records."

Today, she seems to shrug it off. "I can be patient when I need to be," she says, though she points out that she meshes so well in business with her partner and cousin, Rachel Bardis, because "she doesn't get as crazy as I do — I mean in a good way."

I ask if Bardis felt nervous the first time she had to stand before a planning commission and apply for a building permit. "Not really," she says. "I used to go with my dad to a lot of those meetings and all of a sudden he'd just turn to me and tell me to stand up and make the presentation or answer the questions. He kind of forced me to speak up but with absolute love. It gave me confidence because he had a lot riding on how I'd do."

In addition to her project The Mill, which was a bestseller long before it opened, Bardis has a special fondness for The Good Project at Fifth and B streets in West Sacramento (right past the I Street Bridge), which she calls an "energy-conscious infill project."

First envisioned as a "green" community in 2008, The Good Project features homes from 1,200 square feet to 1,900, a price range of $365,000 to $457,000, a community park and a garden. "This concept was ahead of its time," Bardis says, "and completing the homes is like a dream come true for me."

She has other dreams, of course. She says she'd like to build infill, high-density projects in such sprawling cities as Woodland and Elk Grove. She'd like to see an expedited planning review process but also thinks developers should be "incentivized to start building as soon as they get their plans approved and funding in place. Land banking hurts everyone."

Bardis is married to fellow developer Bay Miry and says it helps to have a husband who's in the same business as she is. "When Bay says, 'I've had a rough day,' I totally get it," she says.

March 19, 2018

Doctor and lawyer Viva Ettin has two celebrations in mind

South African native Viva Ettin — physician, attorney and tireless public television booster — celebrated her 40th year in the United States in 2017 and refuses to stop her flag waving. "When you come here as an immigrant, you have no personal infrastructure," she says. "You're standing on a precipice, all alone. Then you find that Americans are waiting for you with open arms — and those arms are what saved me."

Over a lunch of Caesar salad and french fries — at 5 feet, she weighs about 100 pounds, so she must know what she's doing — Ettin spends equal time saluting the red, white and blue and KVIE's annual fundraising bash, which is set for April 8 at the historic Teichert/Downey home, owned by Nancy and Fred Teichert, in the Fab 40s. To salute PBS' signature "Nature" and "NOVA" shows, this year's theme is "Safari." Guests are being encouraged to show up in what I like to call suburban jungle ensembles — you know, immaculately creased tan shirts with epaulets, pleated cargo shorts and scuff-free, water-resistant combat boots with cunning side zippers.

Ettin, who proudly announces she's 63 (I credit the french fries), has helped planned four of KVIE's yearly fundraisers over the past seven years, wooing sponsors with her precise (and often-mistaken-for-British) accent and, above all, her salty sense of humor. At her insistence, you won't find much of the latter displayed in today's column, unfortunately.

She moved to the U.S. from Johannesburg and says "a

piece of my heart will always lie in that big city in the bush." She then quickly adds, "But I love America best. I love you guys. You're such an open people and have shown so much courage." She says she'll never forget the airline passengers on 9/11 "who knew they'd die by taking on the terrorists and still said 'Let it roll.' " She's referring to United Airlines Flight 93, the plane that crashed into a Pennsylvania field.

"So many others could have been killed if they hadn't been willing to give their lives," she says. "This is what America and Americans look like to me. Brilliant!"

"Brilliant" is Ettin's favorite word these days, used to describe things that indisputably are and things that she's simply enthusiastic about. Which would be nearly everything.

Ettin has been with her husband, Dick Rader, a retired and highly respected attorney for 26 years. They met when she did some legal work for Rader's firm and he thanked her with two bottles of fine wine that he strategically delivered in person. The two travel the world together — Rader taught himself Italian, which he's now fluent in — and Ettin also takes a number of trips with pals such as Joyce Raley Teel and Nancy Teichert. She's flown to Greece to attend a Tsakopoulos family wedding and manages to turn up at every society soiree the region has to offer.

She gives all the praise to husband Rader: "I was telling the Teicherts that Dick holds my balloon to keep me stable. And Fred said, 'No, he holds your balloon so you can soar.' Wasn't that a brilliant thing to say?"

March 20, 2018

Sherie Fox-Eschelbach helps clients get IRS compromises

When Vito Corleone famously said in "The Godfather" that he was going to make an enemy "an offer he can't refuse," he had nothing on Sherie Fox-Eschelbach. Her job is making offers the IRS, which can be a lot scarier than a mere mortal, rarely refuses.

Fox-Eschelbach is an enrolled agent (also known as an EA) who's made tax representation and offers in compromise (also known as OICs) her specialty since 2003. She works with people who've become a focus of the IRS and sometimes other tax agencies ("These things often go hand-in-hand," she says.) for everything from delinquent payment of taxes to nonpayment of same. She eventually makes the tax collectors an offer on behalf of her clients, which is essentially this: Please accept this amount of money and/or this payment plan so that my clients may resume their lives and "sleep through the night for a change."

On a recent Saturday over lunch at Rudy's Hideway, the lobster house not far from the Rancho Cordova/Orangevale border, Fox-Eschelbach talks about her work — but also, amusingly, how she tumbled into it. When she was 20, living in San Jose "and needed a job, like in a hurry," a friend found her one at her dad's accounting firm. "I started just by answering phones," she says. "Then, one day, they handed me the tax organizer they'd send to clients. Then they started me on data entry. But after a few weeks I found errors in some of the things I was supposed to enter. They liked that."

She says she developed a strong interest in taxes and tax law but makes one thing abundantly clear: "God, I hate numbers and accounting. Taxes are totally different." While she works for an accounting firm in collections, billing and tax compromises, her own OIC business, which she operates out of her home, has been growing steadily. Most of her work is done by phone and email. That, and the fact that licensed EAs may work in any state, as opposed to CPAs, who must be licensed in individual states, allow her to take on clients near and far. Even so, "If I have a client here in town who's simply not getting his documents to me, I tell him, 'I'll be over tomorrow at 1, have everything ready.' I've been called a bit aggressive."

A friend of mine who's been a client of Fox-Eschelbach twice — and suggested I may be interested in interviewing her — confirms (and marvels at) her tenacity. In an email to me he wrote, "If she takes a person on as a client, she will hound them until they cough up all the detail she needs to help them."

I ask how people get themselves so behind on their taxes, and she says it becomes "a self-perpetuating problem. People hide the problem for as long as they can. They lose sleep. One year of not paying taxes turns into two years, then five. And the notices keep coming. I understand it. And I understand that the hardest thing for them to do is walk through my door or make that call."

She says that 99 percent of her clients — 80 percent of whom are men — "have gone through a major life-changing event. Most of them own their own businesses. Maybe the economy changed and left them behind. Maybe they lost a spouse to cancer. They're good people who need help. And I love to help them. There's nothing better for me than hearing back from the IRS that the offer's been accepted and then making a call to my client to say, 'Guess what we did!' "

Fox-Eschelbach, who's 51, has two grown daughters — and, by the elder of the two, six grandchildren. She's been in a "great relationship" for more than four years. When she isn't working nonstop, she enjoys gathering sea glass — bits of debris that wash ashore or stay just out of reach to make her wade up to her waist — and designing "jewelry and knickknacks. It centers me."

Since I often ask successful people what parental advice inspired them, she laughs. "My mom said to me when I got into this line of work, 'Well, life consists of two things: You pay your taxes. Then you die.' "

March 23, 2018

Meet Dave Toof, popular as a cashier and Google guide

When he isn't cheerily ringing up your groceries at Corti Brothers, the locally famous supermarket and deli for which he's worked 31 years, Dave Toof goes on photo safaris throughout the Sacramento region, using his cellphone to shoot stylish interior and exterior pictures of area businesses.

Toof does this as a Google guide — a member in excellent standing (we'll learn why in a moment) of the unpaid corps of photographers whose pictures, if selected, pop up when you Google, in his case, PetSmart, Panera Bread Store and Taco Bell in Delta Shores; Dick's Sporting Goods; Wal-Mart; Panda Express; and, just across the street from Corti's, El Pollo Loco, H&R Block and Español, the family-style Italian restaurant (forget the misleading name) that's been around since 1923.

That's where Toof and I are sitting this recent rainy afternoon, talking about his superhero origins — a phrase I'm using because he's also a huge fan of George Lucas films and a movie memorabilia collector. He also loves old TV shows and today is wearing a stylish gray jacket reminiscent of the linen numbers Don Johnson used to wear on the first iteration of TV's "Miami Vice." (It's why you can email Toof at janhammerrules@gmail.com. Hammer wrote the show's memorable electronic score.) Customers agree that Toof's the most fashionable person to ever ask you if you want to purchase a bag for your groceries.

It's fun to discover that Toof, a genuine people person, is also a creative loner who puts hours into taking photos of such professional quality. "What makes this fun," he says, "is I'll be driving around and see, for example, a restaurant I've never seen before. I Google it and see if anyone's taken pictures of it. If not, or if they're just not very good, I may go back there in the morning and afternoon and evening to shoot the inside and outside until I get the pictures I want. Then I post them."

On this particular day, a pop-up has appeared on Toof's phone from Google itself, congratulating him on hitting a milestone he's by now surpassed: His photos have received 5,145,055 views. "There are people in L.A. who probably have numbers like 100 million," he says modestly, "but I'm pretty proud of having achieved this locally." He's been doing this for less than a year, it should be added.

While Google doesn't pay for the pictures, the company does offer occasional rewards to its highest-viewed cadre of camera bugs, Toof says, such as books, movies and coupons. He'd love to monetize his avocation, he says, but "I'm not sure how. Corporations hire their own photographers for the official shots of their businesses." As an objective observer, I can tell you that many of Toof's are far superior — and, remember, he's not doing this with an entourage and enough equipment to fill a Winnebago.

Single and a very youthful 50 — "I look like a fetus with shoes," he jokes — Toof is a native of Sacramento and a graduate of Capital Christian School. One of his earlier hobbies was collecting and working on Alfa Romeos —the car Dustin Hoffman drove in "The Graduate" — "but that got pretty expensive." He started his photographic pastime making home movies with his older brother, Glenn, and credits his late cousin Debby, who was 10 years his senior, for taking him under her wing when he was young and encouraging him to experiment with angles and subject matter.

I ask him what the oddest reaction he's received from his walking into an eatery unannounced (and with no Google ID card) and suddenly starting to snap away. He grins. "I was taking photos of the counter with the sauces and napkins in a fast-food place and a woman there asked me, 'Excuse me, sir, do you have an interest in condiments?' I told her what I was doing and showed her, in my phone, some of the other photos I'd done. It turns out she thought I was from the county health department, and she and another employee then spent the whole time I was there cleaning everything like crazy."

Attorney Marcia Augsburger helps clients untangle health care law

"The fact is, clients still tend to respect men more than women," says attorney Marcia Augsburger. "It used to be that even if I explained something to a male judge, lawyer or client, he'd then turn quizzically to any male lawyer close by and ask if I'd been correct — as if I had said nothing at all or he had forgotten his pig Latin. I could have said the same thing (but) only the male lawyer was understood or acknowledged, even if he used exactly the same words I had." At this, she smiles slightly and exhales. "But I'm experienced and old enough now that most men listen to me."

They really should. Augsburger, who'll be 59 next month, has been an attorney for nearly 30 years, specializing in health care law since 1999. An equity partner based in the Sacramento offices of the global law firm King & Spaulding, Augsburger could have pursued — and more to the point, succeeded at — a number of careers other than the law.

She spent four years as a schoolteacher and still has a knack for explaining everything from the mundane to the highly complex with clarity and candor. She's also a visual artist, a musician and a terrific singer.

As you might have guessed, those last things aren't on her attorney résumé. They're personal observations. Augsburger's been a friend of mine for decades, ever since she went to work for McDonough, Holland & Allen — now shuttered but once one of Sacramento's largest law firms — when I was doing its marketing (which I stopped doing long before it shuttered, one hastens to add). She and my late wife, Jane, hit it off as did our two little girls, Lara (hers) and Jessica (ours). Both are now in their early 30s, and Lara gave birth a few months ago to a son, Cashel. So we have some history. (Augsburger's husband and equally lauded law partner at KS Law, Steve Goff, also happens to be a ferocious tennis player. He once beat me playing left-handed, which he wasn't and, to the best of my knowledge, still isn't.)

Augsburger believes her upbringing in the Mennonite church gave her "more grounding than a lot of people grow up with. I've always set high standards for myself but I always knew that if everything failed, I could go home again. It gives me courage."

She still has family in Pennsylvania, notably her parents, themselves overachievers. Her mother, Esther Kniss Augsburger, is in her 80s and remains a prominent artist whose large anti-war sculpture, composed of turned-in guns, has had a few homes, including Washington, D.C.'s Capitol Mall. Her father, Myron Augsburger, is the former president of Eastern Mennonite University, a charismatic speaker and talented writer.

He also has a wonderful sense of humor. At a Christmas dinner at the home of Augsburger and Goff many years ago, he started the meal off by offering a beautiful, compelling grace. I complimented him afterward by saying, "Man, you really ought to do this for a living." He stared at me for a mini-second — it was a tad terrifying, to be honest — then threw back his head and roared with laughter. Only the truly humble can laugh at themselves.

Augsburger says what's been "a very enjoyable focus" for her in the past few years has been on developers of telemedicine products. She advises startup firms on the seemingly unending skein of regulations waiting to entangle them. I ask how a startup can afford a high-proceed firm like hers. "Oh, most of my clients in that field already have their first round of financing in place, so there's really no problem," she says.

Commenting on the challenges she faced as a woman in a once almost exclusively male-dominated profession, Augsburger says she believes that KS Law is "the most egalitarian law firm I've ever worked for — or even seen, for that matter. They think having women as colleagues is simply natural, not something they have to work at pretending it is. I love the environment, and I love my work today more than ever. I can completely lose track of time when I'm at my desk, which is a very good thing — and good for my clients since I bill them based only on the time I track."

Wallrich studio heads east
— to Folsom and Watt

One of comedian Steve Martin's funniest conceptual routines, which also became the title of one of his albums, was "Let's Get Small," a satire of what anxious hipsters might do when they run out of ways to get high.

But it also could serve as the mantra for companies, organizations and empty-nesters either in the confusing throes or enjoying the pleasures of downsizing.

For Lila Wallrich, owner of Wallrich Creative Communications, there's been more pleasure than she anticipated when a few months ago she moved her firm from 5,500 square feet of office space at a trendy midtown address (2020 K St.) to "slightly under 3,000 square feet" at 8801 Folsom Blvd., just off Watt Avenue. At the same time, she trimmed her 16-member staff to eight — but has hired back "most of the people we laid off" for contract work. "I kind of doubled my options by doing this," she says, "because now I have not only people I've worked with before but also a wider pool of subcontractors to call in on certain projects."

In an interview late last week at her new digs, Wallrich looks around and says, "I know this may not be as glamorous an address as before — but never underestimate the joys of free parking!" She's serious about the parking but punctuates the remark with a mischief-making grin — a mock-conspiratorial look that has consistently drawn in (and kept) clients from major players such as Dignity Health, Sacramento Municipal Utility District, American River Bank and the Sacramento Children's Home. I've known Wallrich for a number of years (we served on a nonprofit arts board together and collaborated on a campaign for the city of Sacramento), and she's simply a kick to be with: highly animated, focused and energized, deadly serious about her work but confident enough to bring on the silly.

"Transparent is the only flavor I can do," she says, referring to her passion for candor.

I should point out that the designer in Wallrich wouldn't let any place she hung her chapeau be unglamorous. Original art is hung and strewn throughout the new workplace, and an elegantly patterned carpet runs through it. You may walk onto an immaculately kept but relatively nondescript office campus but when you step into Wallrich's offices, you're in a fast-paced salon.

Twenty-eight years ago today, Wallrich quit a job with another design firm to co-create a firm with Susan Landi, cubbed Wallrich Landi. In 2011, Landi left and Wallrich became the sole owner of her self-named design, branding and advertising agency.

She says that something she's "been loving" about having a smaller full-time staff is that she's personally designing again instead of only supervising. She proudly displays a wooden box of Palomino Blackwing lead pencils, her favorites, that a client gave her. "He just thought it was cool that when he hired Wallrich, the creative design firm, he was also getting Wallrich the creative designer," she says.

May 2, 2018

Animal rescuer Cathryn Rakich fosters one dog at a time

Animal rescuer and activist Cathryn Rakich has her boundaries, she'll have me know. "I only do adult dogs," she tells me. "Puppies are evil."

Rakich says all this with an open-faced cheerfulness — she doesn't really believe puppies are evil (I think) — but wants to make clear that her voluntary, all-but-full-time fostering of dogs in her home a block or two from the American River is a scene of ongoing love, not chaos.

We're chatting one recent afternoon at the city of Sacramento's Front Street Animal Shelter, a bone's throw from the California Auto Museum. Rakich has agreed to meet here because she's decided she may pick up a new foster dog today. Her most recent temporary guest has been adopted, under the shelter's and Rakich's scrutiny, the latter involving a home visit to see what kind of people (and what other animals) will be welcoming the new tenant.

To give you an idea of her world, this is an excerpt from an email Rakich sent me that morning when I suggested our driving to the shelter together and she graciously declined: "I'm going to stop at Western Feed on the way home to pick up a trap to catch a big un-neutered male kitty who has taken up residence in our backyard. Trap, neuter, release. Can't have this big boy out there making more unwanted babies. Plus, there is a chance I'll take home a new foster dog as a result of our meeting ...." She doesn't take home a dog when we meet but after we part, I learn, she gets one from another shelter.

"A lot of strays are brought here," Rakich says. "They're

186

not licensed or neutered. When you adopt them, it's like bailing them out of jail."

She does her work on behalf of Happy Tails Pet Sanctuary — which, if you're an animal lover or even animal liker, you may want to keep in mind during tomorrow's Big Day of Giving. The animal rescue group's been around for 25 years. The organization saves dogs, cats, turtles and rabbits from fates as bad as death, though its predominant clients are cats.

Rakich and her husband, Mark, a chief consultant for the California Assembly's Insurance Committee, have three dogs and four cats of their own. I ask how it goes when she introduces a foster dog into the menagerie, wistfully hoping it's treated like a special guest star. "Well, most of the dogs we get have never really been in a home environment," she says, "so there's a definite period of adjustment. I've had foster dogs for as little as a week and as long as six months. But no matter how long we have one and how attached I feel, our own pets are definitely never disappointed to see one leave."

Animal loving is a lifetime passion for Rakich — and "Mark knew what he was getting into when we first got together. But he's absolutely wonderful about it." Married on New Year's Eve in 2005, they knew when they bought their current home that "the first thing we'd need to do is rip up all the carpets," she says. To maintain some semblance of order, Rakich says she never adopts more than one dog at a time.

Rakich is a vegan, master gardener and "dancercise fiend," she says, whose enthusiasm and energy belie the fact that she'll turn 58 any second now. She won't wear apparel that involves any animal's pain — no leather, no wool and "nothing with feathers, for heaven's sake. Do you know how painful that is for a bird to have its feathers plucked? It'd be like someone pulling out your hair."

If Rakich's name is familiar to you, you probably receive one of the five editions of Inside Publications in which her column, "Pets and Their People," as well as her feature stories appear. To give you an idea of her fan base, when she wrote about my tubby tabby, Osborn the Magnificent, and me in some of last month's editions, I received more calls, emails and arm taps in the ensuing weeks than I often receive for my own newspaper work.

That doesn't bother me one bit. What I may lose sleep over, however, is the notion that puppies are evil.

June 1, 2018

Delta Pick Mello helps California Auto Museum roll on despite the odds

A story in The New York Times on May 11 suggests that venues for classic-car fanatics may be going the way of dinosaurs, IBM Selectric typewriters and Trump attorney Michael Cohen's client list. (Full disclosure: I chose the examples of vanished or vanishing items, not the Times story.)

The news disturbed me because I love classic cars, even though I've never been able to afford to buy, much less take care of one. But I did once own a quasi-classic 1966 Ford Mustang and had planned to give it to my daughter on her 16th birthday — until I drove it home over the Yolo Causeway in a torrential storm 17 years ago and fishtailed so much I just left on my turn signal since I didn't know which way I'd be veering or when. (Shortly thereafter, I donated it to Stanford Home for Children, no doubt for scrap.)

Anyway, the Times story made me decide to visit my pal Delta Pick Mello, executive director of the California Auto Museum, and see how things were going for her and it.

"I showed The New York Times article to my board of directors," she says as we took a quick look at the 72,000-square-foot facility across the street from the Front Street Animal Shelter. I've been to the museum — which officially opened as the Towe Ford Museum on May 1, 1987 — a number of times — but, like many people, almost always to attend an event that had nothing to do with classic cars. Nonprofit and professional groups like to rent the facility because it makes a colorful background for socializing before the guests reluctantly sit down for the usual speeches or awards ceremony or both. "The members expressed their concern but I told them it's what we do differently that helps keep us going," Mello says.

In a nutshell, Mello and her board recognize the fact that gawking at classic cars can provide an aesthetic pleasure and may also ignite a sense of nostalgia. For example, she says, "The AMC Pacer is one of my favorite cars — not because it was super-special even then but because it takes me immediately back to a time when the country was turning to (ownership of) smaller cars. It was in those years that we'd pull into a gas station and, for the first time, I'd see my dad pump his own gas. The world was changing."

Mello, who's been in her current post for two-and-a-half years, says that recognizing nostalgia as a moving target has kept the auto museum relevant since it opened 31 years ago. "I mean, look, I'm 57 years old, so the Pacer has a special place in my heart," she tells me. "For older people, it may be seeing a car from the 1940s or earlier. And younger people are going to think a car from the late 1980s or '90s really takes them back."

The auto museum gets by on sponsorships, admissions, facility rentals and donations, Mello says. She points out that car museums "are notorious" for starting out as personal collections (as this one did). "But when you become a true museum, everything changes: You have to understand and respect a variety of audiences. If you want it to still be here in another 31 years, you have to become a real museum — and that means, changing with the times."

(There's a charming, somewhat personal history of how the museum came to be and evolved — by Dick Ryder, its founder, first CEO and president — at its website: calautomuseum.org/).

Mello herself is a good example of someone not afraid

of change. Prior to taking the steering wheel at the auto museum, she spent eight years working in membership and marketing for the California State Railroad Museum Foundation, a job she took when she left the Sacramento Zoo after 17 years. She has a communication studies degree from California State University Sacramento.

Mello and her husband, Gary, a retired producer and director for news at Fox 40 KXTL-TV — where the couple met when Mello interned there — have two grown daughters: Samantha, 28, who now works for the Railroad Museum, and Clara, 25, who just graduated from the Sacramento Police Academy. Both young women were home-schooled, Mello said. "It wasn't for any religious reason," she clarified. "We just thought we could give them a real grounding" — she smiled almost mischievously — "and allow us to take them on some great trips whenever we wanted to. It was a great learning experience for all of us." But not, I imagine, in an AMC Pacer.

City manager Howard Chan left parking to find his new space

A little more than a year into his three-year contract, Howard Chan has found the perfect parking place, and almost everyone who knows and works with him hopes it won't be a temporary one: He's the city manager of Sacramento.

I'm guessing that Chan is pretty tired of the parking references by now. But when someone's spent most of his career in the parking industry, both in the private and public sectors — he spent 11 years as Sacramento's parking services manager — the allusions may be inevitable. Asked if he ever thought his experience and expertise in parking would lead to his managing the capital city — what Chan calls "a billion-dollar corporation whose services exist for the public good, not to make a profit" — he doesn't even pause before saying, "Never!" It's the only time he raises his voice at our low-key lunch downtown. Then he gives me a genuinely mirthful smile and says, "It's not exactly a position I'd been jonesing for forever."

I mention Chan's smile because it seems interlaced with his style and occasional urban-hipster expressions (e.g., "jonesing," which, as I'm sure you know, means intensely desiring). He makes it a point to do quarterly brown-bag lunches with any of the city's more than 4,500 employees who care to show up ("We average from 100 to 200 each time," he says, "depending on what issues are looming out there"). And, without mentioning the by-now-familiar Tom Peters leadership cliché, he really does manage by walking around — a sometimes dicey proposition when it can involve wading through a crowd of angry protestors beside his hand-picked police chief, Daniel Hahn, after the Stephon Clark police shooting that roiled the city.

"I spent many hours interviewing and just kind of hanging with Dan," Chan says. "I think it's one of the most important hires I'll ever make. And I think the city did very well when we made him chief."

It's been a busy first year for Chan who, despite being so new on the job, has the most seniority of City Hall's charter officers (the handful of employees appointed by the City Council — including the city clerk, city attorney and city treasurer). In addition to the global trauma of the Clark incident and following through on Mayor Darrell Steinberg's much-debated proposal to house the homeless in enormous tents, Chan recently brought a proposed $1.1 billion fiscal year 2018/19 budget to the City Council. It includes a $25 million increase from the current year in general fund operations. "We simply needed to increase our bandwidth," Chan says, "and that meant adding some positions."

Chan is 50 years old and doesn't deny he's a workaholic. He and his wife of 22 years, Emily, have two children: Andrew, 16, and Amanda, 14. His 45-year-old brother, Edmund, a paraplegic as the result of a random street shooting decades ago, also lives with the family in their North Natomas home.

Yet even with such a full plate, if things went according to plan, he participated this weekend in the 27th annual America's Most Beautiful Bike Ride, a fundraiser on behalf of the Leukemia & Lymphoma Society. The event was scheduled to begin and end at the South Shore of Lake Tahoe. He's also taking a Hawaiian vacation with his wife this summer — under specific orders from Steinberg, as it happens.

"He not only told me to take some time off, he called Emily at home and told her to start planning it so that I couldn't back out at the last minute," Chan says, grinning. I bet he'll find a good parking space there.

KCRA's Kellie DeMarco anchors a neighborhood project

A s an anchor and reporter for the past 15 years, Channel 3 KCRA-TV's Kellie DeMarco is accustomed to facing deadlines imposed on her by her professional life — such as the demands of breaking news and the need to strictly adhere to time constraints.

Even so, she's created a deadline for her personal life: to have construction begin this August on the renovation of a children's park deeply embedded in the nostalgic heart of an East Sacramento neighborhood.

DeMarco says that when she first brought her newborn daughter Piper home from the hospital four years ago, "I started looking for places nearby where other new moms took their kids and just hung out with each other."

We're chatting late one recent morning on a bench in East Lawn Children's Park — a block west of the entrance to East Lawn Memorial Park, on Folsom Boulevard at 43rd Street. It's about 11 a.m., and there's a scattering of parents (mainly moms), one or two grandparents and fewer than a dozen kids of various ages, sizes and cultures goofing around on the nearly 30-year-old park's historic but badly aged wooden playground equipment.

The sandbox is littered with a random collection of playthings, and DeMarco tells me, "Take a good look. There's a tricycle with a wheel missing, and other used toys that people just kind of dump here." At night, she says, the park's anemic lighting beckons homeless people to use the facility as an impromptu hostel.

Born in Colorado, DeMarco, who's 38, remembers the

195

importance of her neighborhood park when she was growing up in a residential community called "The Pond" in Arvada County. "Everyone gathered there and everyone watched out for each other's kids," she says. "We need neighborhood parks. We need that sense of community — for our kids now, but also for their kids and grandkids someday."

It's why she's dedicated much of her off-air time the past year to raising funds and friends to give the park a serious makeover. In addition to those who've stepped up and written checks in a range of denominations, area contractors have answered the call, perhaps none as grandly as MarketOne Builders, a commercial contractor that's been donating multiple hours of labor — at a time when the muscular economy would allow it to simply stand still and sift through the projects and offers gusting toward it. (One of its recent high-profile projects was the new B Street Theatre).

In addition, Green Acres, a family-owned and -operated nursery, and Delta Bluegrass, which specializes in sod and low-maintenance lawns, are donating their time, expertise and products to the park's renaissance.

Monday: How to re-grow a park, and everything you want to know about DeMarco. Well, almost everything. Please tune in.

June 18, 2018

Kellie DeMarco — whom we met in Friday's column but probably needed no introduction if you watch TV — may be as well known for her distinctively smoky voice as well as for the two consecutive Northern California Emmy awards she picked up for her anchoring work at the Hearst-owned NBC affiliate KCRA-TV.

She currently co-helms the 6 and 10 p.m. newscasts — and in her off-hours, this single mom is hoping to re-grow a landmark children's playground next door to East Lawn Memorial Park. "I know this sounds like I'm joking," she says as we chat on one of the park's elderly benches, "but East Lawn is donating the sand for the landscaping and sandbox. They have a lot of it."

She's not joking but she does have a mischievous grin. And since people always wonder about television personalities, let's get some of this out of the way.

- She's taller than she looks on TV and is genuine friends both on-air and off-air with everyone on the news team, especially Edie Lambert, who's also a relatively new mom.

- That "beauty mark" on her cheek is quite real, and she says she's had it all her life.

- That smoky voice, which is quite natural (and as compelling in person as on the air), may need medical attention at some point, she says, since lately she's been experiencing periodic voice loss.

DeMarco is co-chairing the hoped-for renaissance of East Lawn Children's Park with longtime area resident and real estate agent, Cindy Leathers, and with support from Sacramento City Councilman Jeff Harris, who was re-elected to office on June 5 with zero opposition. With Harris' endorsement, City Hall has donated $130,000 to the project, but DeMarco estimates it will cost close to $300,000 to make all the improvements — which include new picnic tables, something to shade the sandbox and a variety of toy structures to help kids have tactile adventures.

"Until I got involved in this, I never realized how expensive even a single drinking fountain was," DeMarco says — pausing for effect and then, well, delivering the news: $8,000!

June 21, 2018

Mike Testa really wants you to Visit Sacramento

Mike Testa, president and CEO of Visit Sacramento, is recalling the mini-fracas that broke out a few months ago when the welcoming sign on a water tank as you head into Sacramento — which branded us as the "City of Trees" — was replaced by the current one, which calls us the "Farm-to-Fork Capital."

"I got a lot of calls but only for a few days," Testa says. "One caller, who missed the tree sign, said, 'I'd been looking at that sign all of my life.' And I said, 'Well, then, ma'am, you must be only 16 years old, because that's how long the sign was up.' Then I laughed so she wouldn't feel bad."

It's no surprise that Testa can be hospitable, even when someone's chiding him (and inaccurately, no less). He's been in the hospitality, marketing and public relations industries for decades. And he's been in his current post, for which he has a three-year contract, for the past year, after years of working in "nearly every position at the bureau," most recently as its chief operating officer under Steve Hammond, who retired.

Visit Sacramento's job is to draw conferences and other events here to fill up our hotels, convention center complex and a handful of other venues, as long as they don't arrive for at least 18 months (the convention center books the 18-months-and-under happenings). It used to be known as the Sacramento Convention & Visitors Bureau but a few years ago rebranded itself in what's called (grammar alert) the "imperative mood." Other visitor bureaus throughout the country also have begun doing that. The result, if you

198

respond to ads, is you can't flip through a travel magazine without feeling that all of these cities and states are demanding you visit them — and right away.

While others who happened to be in the room (or building) at the time occasionally take credit for it, Testa is the one who came up with the Tower Bridge dinner, the annual event that you'll always be too late to get tickets to (it sells out in a matter of nanoseconds). It's the A-list part of the region's Farm-to-Fork Festival, a hugely attended local-food fair downtown that also features music and family-friendly activities.

"I've had a couple of fast-food companies try to buy (their way) into the festival," Testa says, "but this really is all about locally sourced food." Interestingly, one vendor that does make the cut is Pizza Guys. "They use Sacramento tomatoes in their products," he says. "It's not easy saying no to some of these other chains because we want to make money, after all." He says the fee for a major vendor can be $25,000.

Tomorrow, Testa explains why the budget for the upcoming convention center expansion has expanded. Visit this column!

June 22, 2018

I t annoys Mike Testa, president and CEO of Visit Sacramento, that much of the outside world thinks his agency consists of city employees. "I don't like it when people say we must not have to work as hard because all of our salaries and benefits are covered by City Hall," he says. "Not true. We aren't part of the city's retirement system, for example. In fact, 82 percent of our funding is private, 16 percent comes from the city and about $125,000 from Sacramento County."

Another $1.67 million, for sales and marketing, comes from the 12 percent-per-room transient occupancy tax, or TOT, which is collected monthly by the city's hotels, along with Sacramento Tourism Marketing District fees, which vary according to where a hotel is situated.

Visit Sacramento and Testa in particular have been in the news a lot lately as the budget for the city's expansion of the convention center complex has, itself, expanded. The Sacramento City Council recently decided to add a large ballroom to the facility. It's also hoping a 24-story, 350-room hotel will be built at the corner of 15th and K streets. "Both of these projects will allow us to attract much larger conventions and to be able to have activities going on simultaneously, as a citywide convention would need," he says. (A citywide convention, he explains, "is one that runs for at least two consecutive nights and utilizes at least 525 hotel rooms.)

Testa says he also wants to bring in more festivals — music, sports and otherwise — "because they help brand the city. State capitals like Sacramento can be at a disadvantage from a perception viewpoint. People may think they're just towns filled with nothing but government workers and they shut down at 5 p.m.

"But look at how Austin, Santa Fe and Nashville have branded themselves as music and art destinations," he continues. "That's what we can do, too, and why the farm-to-fork movement has been so helpful." He points with pride to the fact that the track and field Junior Olympics next year is likely to deposit 7,000 visitors here — and that even with the convention center's renovation causing some disruption for as long as 18 months, "We still have 2,300 hotel rooms in downtown Sacramento and a total of 11,000 between the city and county. We have a lot on the agenda." By comparison, Indianapolis has 12,000 rooms and Austin has 17,000 in their city limits.

Testa admits to being "something of an introvert, which I probably got from my mom," artist Ann Testa, who died in March. But "my dad (Bob) worked as a lobbyist for PG&E and he's very outgoing. I really am a combination of both of them."

He's also a husband and father who turned 49 the day after this interview. His wife, Beth, is a communications consultant who used to work for Edelman, an international public relations firm; the California Rice Commission; and then-state Sen. Mike Thompson (he's now a congressman). The Testas have two young kids, ages 8 and 6. And they, Testa says, are why he loves his work.

"I like being at a New Year's Eve fireworks display that we produce and looking at the enjoyment we provide for multiple generations," he says. "I look at how we're growing as a city and how people think well of us. I want Sacramento to be a place where my kids'll want to stay when they grow up."

Laura Sterner is here for your furry family members

L aura Sterner says that even though she definitely plans to grow her pet-sitting business — in just three years, she already has, almost exponentially — for now, she intends to keep its sphere of influence "hyper-local."

Sterner, 59, currently has "between 30 and 40 clients," none of whom lives far from the home she shares with her husband, Rick, and three dogs in the Arden-Arcade area. She "rarely will do overnights" (staying at the absent owners' homes), she says.

But I can tell you, having used her services twice in the past three months, she delivers more love and care in just one to two visits a day than even some stay-at-home owners provide.

She was recommended to me by Cathryn Rakich. (She's the dog fosterer I wrote about in May who says people still tease her or her husband about her half-kidding remark to me that "puppies are evil.") The fact that I chose Rakich as a reference typifies some of the advice Sterner gave me, to share with you, about choosing a professional pet sitter.

"You should always get as many references as you can," she says over coffee the other day. "People say, 'Oh, I got three.' Well, check out who those three people are. Most of us have three friends we can get to say good things about us."

Sterner says that most of her charges are dogs and cats, but adds, "I've also done fish, lizards and turtles. And if someone had a very exotic pet, I'd look up everything I could about it before I'd consider accepting the job."

She's wired for looking things up. A native of Baltimore

who moved to Washington, D.C., "the absolute second I could get out of Baltimore," she worked in health policy research for the University of California Davis and, in a separate contract, served as assistant managing editor of the Journal of General Internal Medicine, that field's official publication since 1986. (A more fun fact, perhaps, is that she's also a professional bass guitarist. And her husband, who works in information technology at California State University Sacramento, is a professional drummer.)

When Sterner retired from her UCD job, she says she started a web design business, Dare to Dream, but also started pet sitting on the side. "One day I found myself sitting in front of the computer thinking, 'I don't want to be indoors. I want to go see the animals,'" and that's when she made the fulltime commitment to critter care.

"Fulltime" isn't an overstatement. Sterner works seven days a week — after all, people leave town on weekends — and on a busy day "I may make 10 to 15 visits." To care for my own 16-year-old cat, Osborn the Magnificent, she made two stops per day: a relatively brief one in the morning, then a lengthier, cuddle-laden visit in late afternoon. But that wasn't all. Sterner snapped photos of Osborn greeting and eating and texted them to me. It was quite reassuring.

As it happens, "'Reassuring' is a word I've heard a lot since I started doing this," she says. "When I meet the people and the pets, I try to demonstrate that I'm calm and caring but also very professional about this work. What people want most is to know their pets will be safe."

Accordingly, some of her clients authorize Sterner to take their pets to veterinarians should the need arise — and she carries a business liability policy through Pet Sitters International, an educational association.

I ask Sterner if owners, meeting her for the first time, can seem inordinately skittish or hovering. "Well, the only thing that I've had to put my foot down about is the number of multiple visits I'll make while people are deciding on whether they'll hire me," she says. "I'll do one, maybe two, if there's some sort of issue. But when they ask for a third visit, which is like an extended audition, I tell them, sure, but I'll charge them. That usually gets us to an agreement."

Aug. 14, 2018

Nanette Fowler wears many social-service hats

Since Nanette Fowler wears a number of hats, why shouldn't she carry three business cards?

Fowler is the paid CEO of two social services agencies: The Community College Foundation (yes, its name includes "The" and is still a misnomer, as we shall see in a moment); and Shores of Hope (which was named by her talented husband, Chris Terrazas, creative director at the Sacramento News & Review). She's also the volunteer treasurer on the Sacramento Native American Health Center's board of directors.

Fowler has an MBA from Golden Gate University, where she also earned her bachelor's degree in the same area of study, and tells me over lunch that she'd like to get back into doing mixed martial arts. If so, I can't recommend going one-on-one with her. At 44, with a deceptively reedy voice and a sincere belief she's an introvert, she's nevertheless articulate, passionate and tough. If you win her confidence, and I'm guessing that even if you don't, she also allows herself a giggle now and then.

Fowler is known for the financial turnarounds she helped effect at the two nonprofits she now presides over. Asked how she did it — with "only one layoff and (ending) two vacant positions" — she says, "Well, when I came to the foundation, it had (sustained) four years of losses but still had a healthy balance sheet because of its reserves. Pre-me, the foundation sold the building we owned to cut costs and raise money. We're now tenants."

She says she and her staff also "looked at every expense,

with the idea that none was too small to cut. It was all-hands-on-deck: everyone participated. We went line item by line item."

She has a local staff of eight at the foundation, with 50 more at its Los Angeles offices." I ask her if she commutes a great deal between the facilities. "Not really," she says. "We have a weekly conference call, and they all know I'm available by phone at any time. I'm not a micromanager. I think if you treat adults like adults, they'll behave like adults."

Fowler is the very proud daughter (and next-door neighbor) of mom Carol and dad Rick, a retired U.S. Air Force colonel who preceded Nanette in the role as CEO of The Community College Foundation. After starting to put the organization on a firmer financial footing, he was neither in a position to rubber-stamp her hiring nor "would ever have done so," according to his daughter. Rick Fowler is currently chief operating officer of the law firm Kronick Moskovitz Tiedemann & Girard.

The Community College Foundation, which used to be the official arm of the state's community colleges (hence its name), has a $6 million budget and is tasked principally with serving foster youth (mainly in Los Angeles) and running a program called InternSource, which provides paid interns to a variety of client agencies (the interns work for the foundation, which the agencies pay, making the foundation a sort of talent agency).

The foundation also has a mobile classroom, Community Connect, an old bus used for computer training and also to help in disaster relief. The day we speak, Fowler says the converted school bus will be heading to one or more of the multiple fire lines throughout the state to offer assistance to firefighters, residents and pets, a particular passion for her.

206

In addition, the foundation provides back-office support for a number of nonprofit agencies in the region, mainly in information technology.

Meanwhile, after four years as a volunteer, Fowler was asked by the board of Shores of Hope, a $1.75 million organization formerly known as United Christian Centers, to become its CEO. While she juggles both of her jobs whenever the need arises, she actually goes to two different work sites: the foundation is situated in Sacramento's Woodlake region, while Shores of Hope is in West Sac, where Fowler hopes to buy surrounding and proximate lots to expand its possibilities as a provider of housing for the homeless and helping young people make the leap from homelessness and hopelessness to meaningful adulthood.

A few years ago, Fowler was a board member of Happy Tails Pet Sanctuary and says she has had "a lifetime thing about animals." She says she "won't say for the record" how many cats she has at her acre-plus home but clearly knows each by name and personality. I wonder if they also wear hats.

Aug. 16, 2018

Attorney Jackie Sueyres also has a Neat job

J ackie Sueyres is one of those lucky individuals who can say she works for a neat organization.

Sueyres (Soo-AIR-ez) is the owner of Neat Method's first Sacramento-area franchise. The company offers consulting services on how to organize your home, office and/or life. It has satellite franchises in Chicago; Detroit; Miami; Milwaukee; San Diego; San Francisco; Scottsdale, Arizona; St. Louis; New Jersey; and New York.

One afternoon last week I drop in on the Arden Park home Sueyres shares with her husband of four years, Colin, who's the legislative director for state Sen. Jim Nielsen, and their two sons: Fitzgerald, who's 3, and Lincoln, who's just a year old. The little guys are napping when I arrive, and Sueyres' mother-in-law is quietly reading on the patio, presumably ready to spring into grandma action if needed.

I mention this detail along with the fact that the family home, which is around 2,000 square feet but looks larger because of the floor plan, reflects Sueyres' measurable organizational skills.

In addition to its bedrooms, the home has what appear to be two "great" rooms that are neat as a pin, with established "play stations" where the kids can go sketch or paint at an easel, ride some of their (literal) boys' toys or just sit in the middle of the room on the floor if the mood suits them. Everything is in its place — and Sueyres tells me, "They're learning at a very early age to take their toys out but then, when they're through, to put them back." She says the elder boy has even been known to lecture visiting adults should they inadvertently violate this domestic protocol and not return a toy to its place. The family also has two dogs and one cat, but you wouldn't know it when you walk into the home (nor did I meet them during our visit. They might have thought I was too messy for them).

None of this is to suggest that Sueyres or her message is uptight. She's a very down-to-earth businesswoman who also works two-to-three days a week as an in-house attorney for State Farm Insurance. She also hires a sub-contractor to accompany her to most consultations "for safety reasons but mainly because two sets of eyes can be better than one."

Sueyres began the process to purchase her franchise this past March and has been seeing clients just since June. But she says she's already done three jobs (two for home offices), had three additional consultations and is about to start two new projects."

"I've always been organized," she says in a low voice (we're both speaking softly to allow Those Who Must Be Obeyed to continue napping), "and I've always loved reading books about organizing." With a grin, she jokes that her husband "calls my books organizing porn."

I ask her to tell me the biggest mistake people make when they move into a new home or office and want to get organized. "That's easy," she says. "They get overwhelmed. You have to start small, like just with your junk drawer — and believe me, everybody has one. But when you take these little steps, you start to feel good, that you're making progress. And if you're reorganizing an existing space, the first thing to do is to take everything out of the room. Then you start figuring what you really need to keep and what can go."

Shortly before I leave, Sueyres says that Lincoln, the younger, non-lecturing tot, was born on her husband's birthday — barely. "I had an epidural block so wasn't in pain, and I just knew I could hold out another few minutes to make it to Colin's birthday." Sure enough, the baby was born at 12:35 a.m. Now, that's organized.

PASSING THOUGHTS

An anniversary waltz for a memorable day

Forty years ago this morning, the former Jane Turczyn and I were married on a patch of sand in front of the Capitola Venetian, the multicolored units said to be the state's oldest condominium development. I'm commemorating but won't be celebrating the event because Jane died early in 2007 — but with your indulgence, I'd like to use the occasion to tell you a bit about the life we each, then both, discovered upon arriving here separately in the summer of 1976.

Sacramento was certainly no longer a Gold Rush town by then — though in comparison to Chicago, where Jane had spent her early adulthood, and New York City and Southern California, where I grew up, you could still detect the remnants of a rambunctious past. Once we met and began our relationship, we found this encouraging, having both come from rowdy places.

I arrived too late to be aware of (much less involved in) some small scandals at Sacramento City Hall, which mainly concerned people married to other people who were sleeping with people married to other people.

Going to work in local television, Jane could have started her own #MeToo movement in her first week there — it seemed to her that everyone from senior management to news anchors to weathercasters to reporters to camera persons were sleeping with people married to other people. (And when I say, "sleeping," please add the clause "not a wink.")

But that was then, and we were hardly angels

ourselves. Both Jane and I had moved to Sacramento with other partners. Then one day, on one of her first on-air assignments for the TV station, she came to interview me, who'd come up here to work for City Hall, at an official event. And before long, we, too, were people who were sleeping with people who — well, you get the idea. No need to set up the PowerPoint.

The fact that our union lasted so long is perhaps a testament to the belief each of us had that the other one could do much better in terms of finding a life partner. It wasn't false modesty on either side: We were just stunned, for the next 29 years, that we'd lucked into a romance and friendship that stood the test of time, financial reversals, the joyful birth of our daughter (which had been preceded and was to be followed by miscarriages) and ultimately, the nine-year illness that ended with her passing.

When we'd come to Sacramento, and had yet to meet each other, both of us had thought we'd stay about two years, then head back to our respective hometowns. For Jane, that meant returning to Chicago to land a reporting spot on the CBS affiliate, a post she'd been more or less assured would be waiting for her once she got some on-camera experience here (the offer came just a year after she went on the air.) For me, it would be to go to work full-time at the Los Angeles Times, for which I'd freelanced my way into a regular-correspondent gig, or back to my original newspaper job in Long Beach, where the managing editor had talked to me about someday becoming the chief editorial writer.

But once we met we discovered the things Sacramento had to offer: moderate weather, a surprisingly sophisticated art scene, accessible scenic beauty, educated and enthusiastic friends — and most of all, each other. In our situation — far from affluent but not exactly scraping by — Sacramento was also a wonderful place to bring a child into the world. Just before I lost her, Jane had also told me this was the place she wanted her life to end.

I have no idea when or where my own time will come. But I do know that there was and is something vibrant, warm and hopeful about this area. Its collective ethos, services and compassion kept my wife and me together in days and years of duress, and let us relax enough to absolutely gorge on the happy times. What more can you ask of your cherished hometown, even if it's an adopted one?